CATHERINE THE GREAT, CEO

CATHERINE THE GREAT, CEO

7 PRINCIPLES TO GUIDE & INSPIRE MODERN LEADERS

ALAN AXELROD

STERLING
New York

STERLING
New York

An Imprint of Sterling Publishing
387 Park Avenue South
New York, NY 10016

ISBN 978-1-4549-0573-8

Distributed in Canada by Sterling Publishing
c/o Canadian Manda Group, 165 Dufferin Street
Toronto, Ontario, Canada M6K 3H6
Distributed in the United Kingdom by GMC Distribution Services
Castle Place, 166 High Street, Lewes, East Sussex, England BN7 1XU
Distributed in Australia by Capricorn Link (Australia) Pty. Ltd.
P.O. Box 704, Windsor, NSW 2756, Australia

For information about custom editions, special sales, and premium and corporate purchases, please contact Sterling Special Sales at 800-805-5489 or specialsales@sterlingpublishing.com.

Manufactured in the United States of America

2 4 6 8 10 9 7 5 3 1

www.sterlingpublishing.com

Frontispiece: *Portrait of Catherine II* (1763) by Russian painter Fyodor Rokotov (1736–1809).
Picture Credits: ii. Courtesy of Wikimedia Foundation; V. Catherine II of Russia (1729–1796), engraved by R. Woodman and published in *The Gallery of Portraits with Memoirs* encyclopedia, United Kingdom, 1835. © Shutterstock/Georgios Kollidas
Chapter openers: Antique engraved portrait of Catherine the Great of Russia, © iStockphoto/FierceAbin

Cover image: *Portrait of Catherine II* (1729-96) c. 1770 (oil on canvas) by Fyodor Stepanovich Rokotov (c. 1735-1808); Hermitage, St. Petersburg, Russia; Russian. ©Bridgeman Art Library

For Anita and Ian

CONTENTS

Introduction
What's So Great about Catherine?

Since 1999, I have written a dozen books on business leadership, based on some of history's most notable leaders. Of these, *Catherine the Great, CEO* is only the second devoted to a woman leader. The first was *Elizabeth I, CEO.*

The fact is that historians generally cite just two towering woman monarchs, Elizabeth I of England (1533–1603) and Catherine II of Russia (1729–96), invariably comparing the second to the first. That there is such a dearth of writing and research available on historical female leaders is unfortunate both for today's women leaders and for writers in search of subjects that appeal to them. The popularity of *Elizabeth I, CEO*–a *BusinessWeek* bestseller in 2000–attests to the vigorous demand for historical, strategic, female leadership role models. So, after twelve years, it seemed high time for another.

But is Catherine the right one?

She has certainly attracted a great deal of interest, from her own eighteenth century to our twenty-first. Most recently, she has been the subject of a major *New York Times* bestseller biography by Robert K. Massie (2011) and an acclaimed PBS docudrama (2006), but these are just the latest in a long succession of biographies, histories, novels, and biopics, which even include some early silent films.

Except for the most recent works, the majority of books and films devoted to Catherine have hardly focused on issues of leadership. Accounts of her harrowing adolescence and young womanhood in the court of Russia's Empress Elizabeth, her arranged marriage to the psychopathic, profoundly deranged, and ineffably repugnant Grand Duke Peter (later, Czar Peter III), and her love life (more to the point, her *sex* life) have dominated virtually all popular and literary treatments of Catherine, including a surprising number of academic (or at least learned) studies as well.

Certainly, the sex has crowded out everything else in the purely pop culture portrait of Catherine the Great. Even during her own lifetime, Catherine–this empress who seized the throne from her husband and may even have been complicit in his murder–was often portrayed as a nymphomaniac. The scurrilous embellishments became more numerous and sensational as time went on, culminating in the persistent legend that she died trying to appease her sexual appetite by means of intercourse with a stallion. Suspended by a system of ropes and pulleys above her bed (the legend goes), the steed was lowered too quickly and crushed her to death.

Let's clear the air: This never happened.

The empress died of a cerebral hemorrhage, or stroke–at the time called *apoplexy*–and she was alone in her bedroom at the time. It is quite true that she had a lifelong passion for *riding* horses, and, as a superb horsewoman, she defied convention by riding astride rather than sidesaddle. While living in the court of St. Petersburg under the watchful eye of Empress Elizabeth and her many minions, Catherine even invented a unique convertible saddle. It could be configured as a sidesaddle when she set off on a hunt or a ride while Elizabeth and others looked on; and then, far from prying eyes, it could be reconfigured on the fly for riding astride.

She outrode most men. Was there a sexual element in this? Well, she certainly took great pleasure in it. Did she therefore have sex with her horses? No.

As for human lovers, a dozen men have been thoroughly documented, including one she made the king of Poland, one who was her adviser at the highest level, and the redoubtable Grigory Potemkin, who was virtually her consort and may even have been secretly her wedded husband. During her own lifetime, many people in her court and throughout Europe believed she had far more than twelve liaisons–the vast majority with *very* young men. During her own lifetime and afterward, she was the subject of pornographic novels, magazine stories, and engravings. Today, most reputable historians have settled on the twelve documented lovers over the course of some thirty years–a lively but hardly sensational romantic résumé for three decades in the life of a widow.

Of course, disproving nymphomania does not in itself qualify a woman as a leadership role model. Once we have disposed of the sexual canards, we are left with what some have seen as a usurper, turned reformer, turned tyrant. No less a figure than the English poet Samuel Taylor Coleridge celebrated Catherine's passing in his "Ode to the Departing Year," expressing with pleasure his great relief that "No more on Murder's lurid face / The insatiate Hag shall gloat with drunken eye!"

It is true that Catherine presided over two major wars of conquest against the Ottoman Empire. It is also true that, while she started her reign as a reformer–an empress steeped in the Age of Enlightenment and one determined to bring Russia into the family of Western European nations and to exorcise the long-lingering specter of Ivan the Terrible–she later turned her back on reform and on the more liberal aspects of the Enlightenment. The reason for this retreat was the French Revolution. As it did with so many other European sovereigns, that cataclysm, which began in 1789 and lasted beyond her life and reign, struck terror into

Catherine's heart and mind. Fearing infection by the contagion of "Jacobin extremism," anarchy, and mob rule, and loath to share the fate of Louis XVI, Catherine II became increasingly repressive in the last years of her reign. Yet she never crossed the line into outright tyranny.

Her bad years–in the context of Russian history, hardly as bad as most–spanned 1789 to 1796. The progressive years began in 1762. For her last seven years, the best that can be said of Catherine was that she was better than all her predecessors save Peter the Great, though she was still less of an absolutist than he. For more than a quarter century of her rule, however, Catherine amply deserved the rank historians accord her, placing her alongside Austria's Joseph II and Prussia's Frederick the Great as the most exemplary of the Enlightenment monarchs.

The "bottom line" of Catherine's reign was that, like England's Queen Elizabeth I, she left her empire far greater and far more just and humane than she had found it. Like the earlier English monarch, the Russian came to power both as an outsider and as a survivor: an *outsider* not only as a woman in what was overwhelmingly a man's world, but as a contender for leadership who was neither a court insider nor the possessor of a direct right to the throne; a *survivor* because the prospect of coming of age in the literally cutthroat court of Russia (to say nothing of living long enough to become head of state) was a long shot, at best. Finally, like Elizabeth, Catherine leveraged her presumed "liabilities"–her status as outsider, as survivor, and, most of all, as female–to ignite, fuel, and sustain her rise to leadership and to inform all of her leadership decisions.

This said, as was the case with Elizabeth I, Catherine II was finally a *great* leader neither because nor in spite of her being a woman. She possessed and acted upon unisex and universal qualities of intellect, heart, and character that have driven all of history's most successful leaders–an otherwise diverse lot that includes the likes of Julius Caesar, Napoléon, Theodore Roosevelt, Winston Churchill, and Mohandas Gandhi. And as with these other luminaries, her career leaves us a rich documentary record of precisely what went into her most consequential leadership decisions.

Of the fourteen czars and empresses of three centuries of Romanov rule, only two are called "Great": Pyotr Alekseyevich (Peter I, 1672–1725) and Yekaterina Alekseyevna (Catherine II). Peter built St. Petersburg, the magnificent Baltic city that gave hitherto isolated and backward Russia a "window onto the West." Catherine created the equivalent at vast Russia's southern extreme, founding Sevastopol (1784) and Odessa (1794), the great ports of the Black Sea. Peter opened Russia to Western technology and Western principles of government and administration. Catherine introduced the Enlightenment to Russia, including the transformational ideas of Voltaire, Rousseau, and Diderot, as well as the best of European art, literature, and architecture. She revolutionized education in her country; she reformed and rewrote the nation's tangle of medieval laws; she improved the lot of the serfs and the peasants; and she founded orphanages, hospitals, and one of the world's oldest, largest, and greatest art museums: the Hermitage. Indeed, Catherine became the single most prolific collector of art in Europe.

The empress introduced a high degree of religious tolerance to Russia, and she also imported inoculation against smallpox. Peter the Great had made enormous strides toward turning Russia into a formidable military and political power. Catherine built on Peter's achievement to expand the empire–not only in extent and population but also in its international cultural influence. Her leadership broadened the Russian mind and made possible the creative environment that produced the likes of Pushkin, Gogol, Dostoyevsky, Tolstoy, and the many other figures in literature, philosophy, science, and the arts that followed them. Much as Elizabeth I transformed England from an insular backwater to an island that broadcasted its influence and power to the world, so Catherine the Great transformed Russia from what much of the world viewed as a frozen and barbaric wasteland into a realm of profound and far-reaching cultural, intellectual, and political ferment.

Sophie

She was born Sophie Friederike Auguste, princess von Anhalt-Zerbst on April 21, 1729, in what was then the Pomeranian city of Stettin in the kingdom of Prussia and is today Szczecin, Poland. Her father, Christian August of Anhalt-Zerbst, was a prince–a title that sounds far grander than it was. Anhalt-Zerbst was among the least considerable and most provincial of the fragmented fiefdoms and principalities in a Germany that was still far from becoming a nation, let alone an empire. His wife, Princess Johanna of Holstein-Gottorp, was not only younger than he, but she also came from a family of superior position. Holstein was a more cosmopolitan and more considerable duchy than Anhalt-Zerbst–and its ruling family had claim to the Swedish crown. Johanna's great expectations were dashed when her marriage was arranged with Christian August rather than some more brilliant figure. Not surprisingly, she soon tired of her aging husband and her wearisome provincial life, and she took every opportunity to get away, traveling to the estates and castles of the many noble German families to whom she was related.

In contrast to herself, Johanna's brother Charles Augustus had made a spectacular match with Princess Elizabeth Petrovna, daughter of Russia's Peter the Great. Tragically, however, he succumbed to smallpox before the wedding, leaving the bride-elect devastated. Elizabeth's sister Anna, in the meantime, had married Duke Charles Frederick of Holstein-Gottorp. Anna died just three months after giving birth to their son, Peter Ulrich. Ten years later, Charles Frederick also died, leaving the orphaned Peter a claimant to the Swedish throne and, as the only surviving male descendent of Peter the Great, a potential heir to the throne of Russia as well.

The Russian throne was hotly contested. In November 1741, Elizabeth rallied the Imperial Guard–officially the *Leib* Guard, or "Life" Guard–to her cause and overthrew the empress Anna Leopoldovna, who governed as regent for Czar Ivan VI, a year-old infant who was in a highly tentative line of succession rooted in the half-brother of Peter the Great. Having assumed the throne, Elizabeth imprisoned little Ivan and his family in the fortress of Dünamünde and proclaimed fourteen-year-old Peter Ulrich of Holstein-Gottorp her heir. She summoned him to the court at St. Petersburg, changed his name to Peter Fyodorovich, and conferred upon him the title of grand duke.

Elizabeth's next step was to find a suitable match for this future czar, so she turned to the family of her late fiancé. As it turned out, Princess Johanna of Holstein-Gottorp's daughter Sophie was fifteen–close in age to Peter Fyodorovich. The Russian empress sent an invitation to Johanna to promptly accompany her daughter to the St. Petersburg court.

Johanna found the prospect of becoming the mother-in-law to the Russian czar and living as part of a glittering imperial court intoxicating. That her husband, Sophie's father, had pointedly *not* been invited was no obstacle to her accepting the summons; in fact, it was a further incentive to accept. Besides relishing time away from Christian August, Johanna knew his staunch adherence to the Lutheran Church would serve as an obstacle to a match between Sophie and Grand Duke Peter. For her part, Sophie was much closer to her warm and loving father than to her perpetually critical mother. Though she intensely regretted leaving her father, Sophie was eager for adventure.

En route to St. Petersburg–they set off in midwinter, on January 10, 1744–Sophie and her mother paid their respects to Frederick the Great in Berlin. Despite the hardships of the long, laborious, and bitterly cold journey, Sophie discovered a love for travel that would serve her well when she became empress of an empire as vast as Russia. Besides, the discomfort of the trek made both travelers appreciate all the more the luxury Empress Elizabeth afforded them when, at the Russian border, they were met by a magnificent convoy of Imperial sledges that conveyed them to St. Petersburg in the highest style.

Their arrival in that severely beautiful city proved anticlimactic when they discovered that the court had taken up residence for the season in Moscow. Eager to participate in the celebration of the grand duke's sixteenth birthday, mother and daughter set off again, arriving at Moscow, after a journey of some four hundred miles, just in time for the February 10 festivities.

The welcome they received seemed wonderfully auspicious. Empress Elizabeth took an instant and obvious liking to Sophie, who was (as everyone except her own mother seemed to recognize) a pretty, spirited, and extraordinarily intelligent young woman. Grand Duke Peter was also cordial–although he was hardly the model of young manhood both Elizabeth and Sophie might have wanted. The lad was sickly, both in fact and in appearance, looking childish rather than adolescent. He seemed both emotionally and intellectually vacant and may even have been developmentally disabled. How much of this was due to genetics versus having grown up a neglected and largely unloved orphan is impossible to know. Beyond dispute was his attachment to dolls and toy soldiers, as well as a streak of cruelty, which included the abuse of servants and the torture of animals. Apparent at his first meeting with Sophie and Johanna was his profound disdain for Russia and his intense longing to return to his native Holstein-Gottorp. He clung stubbornly to all things Prussian, including piety to the Lutheran religion and a slavish adoration for Frederick the Great. Nevertheless, the affection-starved boy was clearly happy to have Sophie nearby, if only to serve as a playmate.

Whatever her misgivings about Peter, Sophie was determined to fit in at court and among the people of that strange new country. She threw herself into the study of the Russian language and was thoroughly tutored in the Orthodox religion. Her aim: to please her mother, to please the Grand Duke Peter, and, above all, to please the empress Elizabeth. Realistically, at the outset of her sojourn in the St. Petersburg court, she believed that pleasing her mother was probably impossible. Making Peter happy was a difficult objective, but doable–or so it seemed at first. Satisfying the powerful empress, oddly, appeared to be the most fully attainable of all three goals. Within a dishearteningly short time, however, Sophie would come to realize that both the first and second objectives were quite beyond her, and that the best she could hope to achieve with Elizabeth was continual appeasement.

Catherine

Although it was clear to Sophie that Grand Duke Peter was far more interested in playing with his toy soldiers than in courting–or even conversing–with her, she readily accepted admittance into the Orthodox Church on June 28, 1744, and was betrothed to Peter the next day, taking a Russian name and becoming Grand Duchess Yekaterina (Catherine) Alekseyevna.

Although now second only to the empress in rank among women, Catherine saw herself beset by rivals and by Elizabeth's spies. To make matters worse, shortly after they were betrothed, Peter contracted measles, followed by smallpox. Unattractive to begin with, he emerged from these illnesses emaciated, pockmarked, and nearly bald. He drowned his sorrows in vodka, became verbally if not physically abusive, and ostentatiously flirted with other women. After repeated postponements, he and Catherine were finally married on August 21, 1745. Not only was the match loveless, it was (most historians believe) unconsummated.

Catherine felt alone–especially after Elizabeth forced her mother to return to Zerbst–and under impossible pressure. She realized that, as far as the empress was concerned, she had but one purpose in life: to produce an heir. Yet how could she? The grand uke was emotionally disinclined to intimacy with her and apparently physically averse to it as well. In her despair and loneliness, she turned to voracious reading, concentrating on the works of Plato and other classical philosophers, the Greco-Roman historian Plutarch, and the philosophical, political, and scientific works of Voltaire, which would later be followed by those of the younger authors of the French Enlightenment, Denis Diderot and Jean-Jacques Rousseau. While her reading developed her mind and laid the foundation on which she would later build her reign, it further alienated her from Grand Duke Peter, whose meager intellect was too limited to understand such literature.

Months, then years passed. As might be expected, Elizabeth blamed Catherine for her failure to produce an heir. She was subjected to repeated examination by a series of physicians, but ultimately it was Peter who was operated on when it was discovered that he suffered from phimosis, a condition in which the penile foreskin is abnormally tight, making intercourse very painful. After circumcision, Peter was reportedly able to have normal sexual relations. Indeed, soon after the procedure, Catherine became pregnant, and on September 20, 1754, she gave birth to a son, whom Elizabeth named Paul. Later, the grand duke told members of the St. Petersburg court that the child was not his, though he never officially disclaimed him. To this day, many historians believe that Paul–Pavel Petrovich–who would become Czar Paul I, had been fathered by Sergei Saltykov, one of Catherine's early court "favorites."

Catherine was not permitted to mother her son. The empress Elizabeth raised him in her own palace apartments, allowing him contact with Catherine only rarely. It was now crystal clear to Catherine that, as far as the empress was concerned, her role in the Russian Empire had been played and was now concluded. She had created a czar, and there was really nothing else for her to do.

A Covert Life

Bereft of her infant son, Catherine underwent a transformation. She realized she could neither trust nor rely on anyone in court and embarked on what can only be described as a kind of covert life. Outwardly, she did all she could to please–or rather, appease–the empress, and although Grand Duke Peter took every opportunity to insult, offend, and humiliate her, often taunting her with discussions of his extramarital affairs and sometimes physically threatening her, Catherine refused to retaliate. She always stood her ground; no matter the provocation or threat, she would not be intimidated by her husband. In fact, she advised him on governing Holstein (his duchy), and she even personally attended to the administrative details–something for which he had neither interest nor capacity. Out of view, stealthily, she engaged in romantic affairs and accumulated some powerful friends, including the British ambassador, Sir Charles Hanbury Williams. One of the ways the empress Elizabeth sought to ensure her control of Catherine was by severely limiting her allowance. Through Sir Charles, however, Catherine was able to obtain what she called "loans" from Great Britain, quietly circumventing the empress.

Sir Charles was recalled to London at the outbreak of the Seven Years' War in 1756, when Britain sided with Prussia against Russia. If this turn of events was a blow to Catherine, it was even more devastating to Peter, because he could not stand the thought of his despised Russia warring against his idol, Frederick the Great. Into the chaotic situation came Lieutenant Grigory Orlov, who guarded a certain Count Schwerin, formerly Frederick's aide-de-camp, and now, having been captured in battle, a prisoner of war. As Catherine fell in love with the dashing young Orlov, Grand Duke Peter took as his mistress Elizabeth Vorontsova, the niece of Empress Elizabeth's vice chancellor.

Czar Peter III

Whereas Catherine's romance with Orlov was conducted in secret, Peter flaunted his affair. In the meantime, Elizabeth largely neglected her empire and let the conduct of the war drift. On Christmas day of 1761, after suffering a series of apparent strokes, she died at age fifty-three. Peter, who had never shown any affection for Russia, ascended the throne as Peter III. His first major act was to sign, on April 24, 1762, a peace treaty with Prussia that returned to Frederick the Great all of the formerly Prussian territories Russia currently occupied. It was more than Frederick had expected–or even asked. In Russia, the army, which had won the territories at great cost and sacrifice, was outraged to the point of mutiny. The new czar added insult to injury by decreeing a radical change in the traditional Russian uniforms to emulate the style of the Prussians. Moreover, Russian officers were to be schooled in Prussian discipline and the enlisted ranks trained accordingly. Peter III was making the Russian army Prussian.

Coup d'État

To Catherine, it became clear that, one way or another, the reign of Peter III was doomed. If he managed to stay in power, the empire would decline. If he continued to alienate the army, however, the likelihood of his remaining on the throne was slim. Were she to stand by him, she would suffer whatever fate befell him. There was no question of love between them, but she did feel some loyalty–until she caught wind of rumors that he intended to end his marriage with her so that he could make Elizabeth Vorontsova his wife. Catherine realized she now faced an immediate issue of life or death–*her* life or *her* death.

There was something else coming to Catherine's awareness. Grigory Orlov and his brothers, along with Princess Catherine Dashkova–Elizabeth Vorontsova's sister but a fervent admirer of Grand Duchess Catherine–and others, were planning a coup d'état. Catherine would have to decide whether or not to join them, but before she could make the decision, one of the conspirators had too much to drink, spoke out disparagingly against the czar, and was arrested. Fearing that this Captain Passek, under torture, might betray them all, the conspirators decided to act immediately. On June 28, Grigory Orlov's brother

Aleksey evaded guards posted to watch over Catherine, who was staying at Mon Plaisir, the *dacha* ("summer house") at Peterhof, while the czar was at the royal estate in nearby Oranienbaum. Aleksey Orlov arrived at Mon Plaisir at five in the morning, awakened Catherine's maidservant, and sent her to rouse Catherine. He then entered and revealed the conspiracy in detail.

Catherine wasted no time in making her decision. Arraying herself in the mourning dress she still wore–Elizabeth had been dead just six months–she slipped away with Aleksey. Down the road, they were met by Grigory, who took them to the headquarters of the Ismailovsky Regiment of the Life Guard. Descending from the rather shabby carriage the Orlovs had hired, Catherine took charge.

"I have come to you for protection," she told the guardsmen. She explained that the czar was about to arrest her. "I fear he intends to kill me."

At this, the soldiers closed in, knelt down, kissed her hands, kissed the hem of her black dress, and pronounced her their savior. Immediately, the regimental chaplain, cross held aloft, administered to the men an oath of allegiance. From the assembled regiment, the commanding colonel, Count Cyril Razumovsky, strode forward and fell to his knees before the young woman.

Escorted by the regiment, Catherine was conveyed to the Semenovsky Barracks, where more of the Russian army rushed eagerly to her side. Thus augmented, the procession advanced to the great Cathedral of Our Lady of Kazan, where she and Peter had been married. Catherine was overwhelmed to find the cathedral already thronged with the faithful. She was ushered to the altar, where she swore the oath as empress of all the Russias.

What had begun as a secret conspiracy now burst into public with peals of bells and the frenzied huzzahs of the people of St. Petersburg. Thus propelled, Catherine mounted her carriage and rode on to the Winter Palace, where members of the Senate and the Synod were already awaiting her arrival, prepared to swear *their* allegiance to the new empress. Count Nikita Panin, her son's tutor and a longtime ally, brought Catherine eight-year-old Paul. Reunited with the boy, Catherine retired to compose a manifesto, which was rushed into print that very night and handed out on the streets of St. Petersburg.

"It has been clearly apparent to all true sons of our Russian Fatherland that the State of Russia has been exposed to supreme danger by the course of recent events," the manifesto began. Writing now as "Catherine II," the newly proclaimed empress explained that "our . . . Orthodox Church has been . . . exposed to the most extreme peril" by Czar Peter III's adherence to Lutheranism. It cited the subjugation of Russia to Frederick II by a treaty that "trampled underfoot" the "glory of Russia." It spoke of the complete disruption of "internal order, on which the unity and welfare of our entire country depend." And it concluded: "For these reasons we have found ourselves compelled, with the help of God, and in accordance with the manifest and sincere desire of our faithful subjects, to ascend the throne as sole and absolute sovereign, whereupon our loyal subjects have solemnly sworn us an oath of allegiance."

As Catherine's manifesto was being distributed, Peter III received word that she had been proclaimed empress. Those with him at Oranienbaum attempted to persuade him to march against the usurper in St. Petersburg. He refused, but agreed to hole up at Kronstadt, an island fortress in the Gulf of Finland, a dozen miles west of St. Petersburg. Here, Peter had already gathered troops to advance against Danish forces over possession of Holstein territory.

Catherine, however, had stolen the march on her erstwhile husband. Admiral Ivan Talyzin had already secured Kronstadt with a naval flotilla. Peter sailed for Kronstadt, and, finding the entrance to the fortress closed by a boom, climbed down into a small boat and was rowed to the fortress. His intention was to order the boom opened to admit passage of his galley.

A guard called down from the fortress ramparts warning the boat to clear off or the cannon would open fire.

"Don't you know me?" Peter III bellowed in return. "I am your emperor!" With that, he opened his cloak to reveal his uniform and the Order of St. Andrew he wore.

"We no longer have an emperor," the guard shouted back. "Long live the empress Catherine II! . . . Another move forward and we fire!"

Peter ordered his oarsmen to row back to the anchored galley posthaste. Boarding the ship, he suddenly fainted into the arms of Elizabeth Vorontsova, leaving eighty-two-year-old Field Marshal Münnich to decide on the next move. It was to sail for Oranienbaum. By the time the galley anchored there and Peter disembarked, the stunning news was waiting for him: Catherine II was on the march, with fourteen thousand troops.

Indeed, she was not escorted *by* those soldiers, but leading them, mounted on a white charger (see "Lead the March" in Chapter Six). Peter responded by collapsing again, this time on a couch. Upon reviving, he wrote a letter to Catherine, apologizing for his bad behavior, pledging to do better in the future, and offering to share the throne with her. After handing the document to Prince Alexander Golitsyn, his vice chancellor, he ordered him to deliver it to his wife.

Golitsyn dutifully rode out and encountered Catherine and her troops on the road to Peterhof (they did not yet know that Peter was still at Oranienbaum). Hailing the procession, Golitsyn handed the empress Peter's letter. She read it, then returned it to Golitsyn, explaining that the good of the state demanded that she continue the advance and that she would therefore not reply at present. Golitsyn offered no protest. Instead, falling to his knees, he immediately offered to swear his allegiance to her.

In the absence of Golitsyn's return with a reply from Catherine, Peter sent another message via another messenger, General Izmailov. In this one, he abjectly offered to abdicate, subject to the single condition that he and Elizabeth Vorontsova be permitted to retire unmolested to Holstein. To this message, Catherine replied that she would accept the offer–provided that the abdication was put in writing. The general carried this condition back to Peter, who immediately wrote out and signed an abdication, "forever renouncing"–"before God"–the "throne of Russia."

Frederick the Great would later write of Peter III, "He allowed himself to be dethroned like a child being sent to bed."

Indeed, the coup was bloodless, at least up to the point of its consummation. But Catherine did not simply allow her estranged husband and his mistress to take flight out of Russia. On June 29, she ordered him confined, under guard, to an estate in the village of Ropsha. On June 30, she made her triumphal entry into St. Petersburg and accepted the accolades of the masses (see "Sell Selflessness" and "Answer Why" in Chapter Six). On July 6, she learned that Peter was dead–presumably murdered by Aleksey Orlov, although he never unambiguously confessed, and the full circumstances have never been uncovered. The next day, July 7, Catherine issued a manifesto concerning his demise, which she ascribed to "hemorrhoidal colic." It is doubtful anyone believed that diagnosis, but no one much cared. She chose not to attend the funeral.

Enlightenment

Catherine herself knew how fragile her position really was. She resisted the temptation to clean house and instead retained many of the administrators and statesmen who had been active under Elizabeth and Peter III, including both Vorontzovas. She was also under no illusions about the state of the empire–especially its catastrophic finances and its unsustainable social situation. The most urgent problem, however, was the military, most members of which had gone unpaid for some eight months.

Between them, Elizabeth I and Peter III had left the affairs of the Russian Empire in chaos. Even the most basic information concerning the nation was simply unavailable. Catherine was able to get a figure for the treasury deficit–17 million rubles–but no one could tell her anything about revenue. She knew Russia had about 100 million people, but no one in the Senate could answer her simple question, "How many towns are there in Russia?" When she suggested that the senators consult a map, they replied that they had never seen one. At this, Catherine withdrew five rubles from her own purse, handed them to a clerk, and sent him down the street to the Academy of Sciences to purchase the latest map of Russia. When he returned with it, she asked him to count the towns and make a report.

It was quintessential Catherine. She was immersed in Enlightenment theories of government, but she always strove to make practical, actionable decisions. Confronted with a problem, she began by ascertaining the facts and facing the truth, whatever it was. Her wide reading in classical literature must have acquainted her with the legend of the Gordian knot. Tied by Gordius, king of Phrygia, it was universally believed impossible to untie–except by the future ruler of Asia. Alexander the Great approached it, drew his sword, and promptly severed it in a single stroke.

Catherine resolved to bring Russia into the Enlightenment that was sweeping Western Europe. She was convinced that this was her long-benighted empire's only route to salvation, greatness, and glory. As for repairing the empire's economy, she resorted first to what she perceived as its greatest asset: the land. She worked to reform land ownership, agricultural production, and production in the extractive industries–that is, mining. In these enormous efforts, she worked hands-on, from early in the morning until late into the night. As she had done in the case of counting towns, she began by getting the facts. She recruited agricultural experts to study conditions throughout the realm, to report on them, and then to make recommendations for increasing productivity. She looked to the West for the many new types of labor-saving, production-increasing farm machines that were being made there, especially in Great Britain. She ordered their importation en masse.

Catherine thoroughly studied issues of population and demographics. Concluding that Russia's urban areas were overpopulated–a condition that contributed to epidemic disease and put an intolerable strain on local resources–while vast interior regions were underpopulated and therefore underproducing, she launched ambitious advertising campaigns to attract immigrant settlers from the West. She focused particularly on the fragmented German states, where she knew poverty was widespread and opportunity scarce. Before long, the Russian interior began to fill.

With the agricultural situation in hand, she devoted herself to the study of Russian mining. Again, her first step was to achieve enlightenment. She founded a School of Mines in St. Petersburg–the first not only in Russia but also the world. The school even included its own mine, where students were given practical experience and training. At the same time, she recruited and dispatched teams of geologists throughout the country. Their task was to identify promising sources of mineral wealth, especially silver, which was urgently needed to bolster Russian currency. And in her relentless hunt for Russian natural resources, she did not neglect the most traditional of Russian commodities: fur. Under Catherine, the long-established Siberian fur industry exploded into unprecedented profitability.

Even as she began to address agriculture and mining, Catherine also turned to manufacturing. She saw that all the empire's factories were jammed into the big cities, especially Moscow and St. Petersburg, spawning squalid slums in their vicinity. Accordingly, she decreed that no new factories could be built in the two capitals, but that anyone, peasants included, could set up a factory anywhere else. She provided particular incentives to build them in the most underpopulated provincial towns. Soon, small manufactories sprang up throughout the empire. As the years went by, Catherine began to focus as well on the larger factories, and she imported experts from the West to advise owners on designing, building, and operating these facilities. During her long reign, the number of major factories increased threefold, from under one thousand to more than three thousand plants.

Nor was Catherine content to improve only Russian domestic industry. She also sought to open up her empire to world trade to an unprecedented degree. Once again, she called in foreign experts. She also signed a series of trade treaties and, most importantly, ended the long-established practice of levying duties on exports. With this major impediment to international trade taken down, investment in export industries skyrocketed. By 1765—year three of Catherine's reign—the 17-million-ruble treasury deficit had been turned into a modest surplus.

As the Russian economy improved, Catherine instituted a campaign to improve the empire's primitive infrastructure. Roads and bridges were built or repaired. In cities, massive and ruinous fires were a chronic problem. Catherine launched ambitious campaigns to rebuild major urban areas—with ramshackle Moscow at the top of the list—using masonry instead of wood. She saw to the construction of new hospitals, orphanages, and prisons, as well as to the rehabilitation of existing institutions. Determined to train more doctors for the empire, she radically reformed medical education, and she introduced into Russia smallpox inoculation, which, though controversial, was being increasingly adopted in the West. She even set the example for her people by submitting to inoculation and by insisting that her son and heir, Paul, be inoculated as well. In the second year of her reign, 1763, Catherine founded the empire's first college of medicine. The institution was to train medical professionals, including physicians and apothecaries, with emphasis on creating a cadre of competent medical personnel to serve in the provinces. Legislation promulgated in 1775 required every provincial capital to build a hospital and each county of twenty- to thirty-thousand inhabitants to support a doctor, a surgeon, an assistant surgeon, and a student physician.

Catherine recognized that her empire's single greatest untapped resource was its people. She set about making a sweeping reform of education. Again, her approach was hands on. She herself wrote primers and textbooks, and she personally drew up and promulgated a Statute for Schools for all of Russia. A program of state-sponsored public education that would have been innovative in any country at the time, the statute prescribed that every district town (the equivalent of a county seat) build and fund a "minor school" with at least two teachers, whereas every provincial town was obliged to found a "major school," consisting of at least six teachers. Although Catherine was also interested in developing higher education, she held off establishing any new Russian universities–except for medical schools–for the simple reason that she understood her empire lacked the professors to staff them. Instead, she funded scholarships for deserving students to study abroad at the great universities of Western Europe.

Catherine not only introduced the most advanced Enlightenment thought into Russia, she also imported a vast quantity of Western European art, employing both Voltaire and Diderot to advise her on which works to acquire. In this way, she became the most prolific art collector in the world. By the end of her reign, she had purchased nearly four thousand European masterworks, which she housed in the Winter Palace and associated structures, the palace complex begun by Peter the Great and to which she added. Today, the Hermitage, as the complex is collectively known, is one of the world's largest and oldest art museums, and her acquisitions constitute the core of the museum's vast collections.

If, in the eyes of history, Catherine ultimately fell short as a reformer, it was due to her failure to abolish serfdom. She personally abhorred slavery, but she believed that the Russian economy was so dependent on serf labor and that the social standing of the nobility was so inextricably bound to ownership of serfs, that to suddenly end the institution would bring about the collapse of the empire. By way of compromise, she did what she could to ameliorate the condition of the serfs, including enacting decrees and legislation to mandate humane treatment and to require, in the case of nonagricultural serfs, negotiated wages.

Imperial Expansion

Like Peter the Great, who reigned from 1682 until his death in 1725, Catherine greatly expanded the Russian Empire. Peter had established St. Petersburg in the north as his "window on the West." Catherine pushed toward Western Europe in the southern extreme of Russia, at the expense of the Ottoman Empire.

The Russo-Turkish War of 1768–1774 inflicted catastrophic losses on the Turks and obtained for Russia the Crimea and southern Ukraine, along with access to the Black Sea, which made Russia the greatest power in the region. Odessa, the great port of Sevastopol, as well as other important Russian cities were rapidly established following victory in this war. Catherine formally annexed the Crimea in 1783, provoking in 1787 a second Russo-Turkish War, which ended victoriously in 1792. The Treaty of Jassy between the Russians and Turks legitimized Russia's possession of the Crimea and added the Yedisan region to the empire.

In addition to expansion by conquest, Catherine engineered in 1764 the placement of a court favorite and former lover, Stanisław Poniatowski, on the Polish throne (see "Be a King Maker" in Chapter Four). This laid the foundation for three successive "partitions" of Poland, by which that nation was effectively dismembered and divided among Russia, Prussia, and Austria.

Her conduct of the wars of expansion led her to forge an extraordinary working relationship with Grigory Potemkin (1739–1791), who served as her top general, her principal adviser, and her lover and intimate of longest duration. At the height of Potemkin's influence, he was Catherine's virtual consort–some historians believe they were even secretly married. Instrumental in the physical expansion of the Russian Empire, Potemkin was without doubt the most important *man* in the country.

Continuity and Retreat

As soon as her son, Paul, was of marriageable age, Catherine threw herself into arranging a union that would ensure the continuation of the line of succession she had established. After Paul's first wife died in childbirth, along with her child, Catherine wasted no time in making a second match (see "Accelerate and Facilitate" in Chapter Three). By 1776, she was confident that the succession had been assured.

That year, of course, also brought news from North America that the thirteen united colonies of Great Britain had declared themselves the thirteen United States of America, independent from the British Crown. As Catherine saw it, the events across the Atlantic were remote, but the outbreak of the French Revolution thirteen years later was quite another matter. Like other European monarchs, Catherine II viewed it with shock, horror, and fear. The increasing intensity of the French Revolution, culminating (for Catherine) in the executions of Louis XVI and Marie Antoinette in 1793, drove her to retreat from her long embrace of Enlightenment ideals of governance. The final seven years of her thirty-four-year reign were marked by a degree of repression that echoed–but by no means duplicated–the autocratic tyranny of her predecessors.

Legacy

For many, Catherine's political and philosophical retrenchment late in her reign indelibly mars her legacy. In this book, however, I suggest that, without overlooking the end of her life and career, we focus on the far longer portion of both, in which she brought to

Russia the Enlightenment as well as her enlightened leadership. In an autobiographical epitaph composed about 1791, Catherine herself outlined the legacy for which she wanted to be remembered:

HERE LIES CATHERINE THE SECOND

Born in Stettin on April 21, 1729.

In the year 1744, she went to Russia to marry Peter III. At the age of fourteen, she made the threefold resolution to please her husband, Elizabeth, and the nation. She neglected nothing in trying to achieve this. Eighteen years of boredom and loneliness gave her the opportunity to read many books.

When she came to the throne of Russia she wished to do what was good for her country and tried to bring happiness, liberty, and prosperity to her subjects.

She forgave easily and hated no one. She was good-natured, easy-going, tolerant, understanding, and of a happy disposition. She had a republican spirit and a kind heart.

She was sociable by nature.

She made many friends.

She took pleasure in her work.

She loved the arts.

The Outsider, the Survivor, the Insider

CATHARINE II. ALEXIEVNA. EMPRESS OF RUSSIA. REIGNED XXXV YEARS.

Lesson 1
Lead with Gentleness and Reason

> "All my life I have had this inclination to yield only to gentleness and reason—and to resist all pressure."
>
> ~ *Memoirs*, 1759–1794

As a girl growing up in Germany, the future Russian empress was tutored by a narrow-minded pedant known to history only as Pastor Wagner. He taught by rote and drill. He discouraged curiosity and questions. He substituted authority for reason. And he underscored every lesson with shouts and a brandished cane.

What did Catherine learn from this?

First, "I am convinced in my inmost soul that Herr Wagner was a blockhead." Second, that truth is arrived at through "gentleness and reason," not coercion and the pressure of arbitrary authority, no matter how fearsome.

Although destined to be an "absolute ruler," Catherine nevertheless believed that truth—and genuine authority—was the product of reason and had to be evaluated by the standards of reason. She would never rely on such doctrines as the "divine right" of kings or on mere repressive force to assert her authority or to maintain her throne. Instead, she sought to lead through reason, with the promotion of the nation's welfare as her constant objective.

> **Authority does not** emanate from an official title, and leadership cannot be sustained by arbitrary coercion. It must be earned—daily—through gentleness and reason.

Lesson 2
Believe You Need Everyone

> "No one was neglected by me, and I made it a rule to believe that I needed everyone and as a result to act in such a way as to win their goodwill . . ."
>
> ~ *Memoirs*, 1759–1794

Princess Sophie had come to the Russian court of Empress Elizabeth a stranger in a strange land. Her own mother treated her coldly, as did many others. Sophie was anguished and, even more often, bored. But, she wrote in her memoirs, "I kept myself from talking about it." When one of the court ladies saw Sophie crying one day, she asked about her tears. "I gave her the best reason [for them] I could, without telling her the true ones." She believed that betraying her misery would make others dislike or even shun her, and her objective was "more than ever to gain the affection of everyone in general, great and small." In this way, she planned to build a world for herself and to ensure that she occupied a central place within it.

While rising within an organization requires identifying those who have the power to help you, this must never be done at the expense of others. Your best chance of succeeding within any community is to embrace everyone and to neglect no one. Make it a personal rule to believe, sincerely, that you need everyone. Act in strict accordance with this belief.

■

Lesson 3

Conceal, but Don't Evict, the Devil of Pride

> "[My mother was determined] to drive the devil of pride out of me."
>
> ~*Memoirs*, 1759–1794

By nature, Sophie Friederike Auguste of Anhalt-Zerbst–the future Catherine II of Russia–was an independent, willful, rebellious, even arrogant child. At least, this is how her mother, Johanna Elisabeth, princess of Holstein-Gottorp, thought of her. Were she to be evaluated by modern standards, it is more likely that Sophie's independence would be considered a positive trait. She would be characterized as a "spirited" child.

Johanna did not see it this way. She did everything she could to break her daughter's spirit, "to drive the devil of pride out of her," as Catherine recalled her mother's phrase. The result was not a broken child, but, rather, one who learned early in life to be crafty and canny. The future empress of Russia learned not to abandon her pride, but deliberately to mask it with a persuasive show of humility and deference. This, in fact, became for her the equivalent of a turtle's shell. Whenever she felt herself threatened–or whenever she needed the time and space to evaluate a new person or situation–she deliberately withdrew into the pose of humility.

The strategic and tactical cultivation of humility was not something young Sophie had to fashion from whole cloth. She was fortunate to have as a governess a French Huguenot refugee named Elizabeth "Babet" Cardel, a woman as gentle and open as her tutor, Pastor Wagner, was harsh and narrow-minded. Cardel, Sophie came to understand, had been born to some degree of rank and privilege, but, as a refugee from religious persecution, she had been forced to accept the position of governess, a family servant. She played the role consummately, Sophie observed. Cardel demonstrated that she knew her place, but she never became servile. On the contrary, Sophie saw in Babet Cardel an essential pride with which she deeply identified. Her example taught Sophia that it was possible to play a role, in order to obtain what you needed without sacrificing your core self.

Our parents tell us—as we in turn tell our children—to "be yourself." Although this sounds like self-evidently valuable advice, it may be high time to question it. You need not present a single face to all those with whom you interact. Colleagues, bosses, subordinates, customers, vendors, clients, investors—each wants something different from their relationship with you. Learn to manage the presentation of your identity strategically, in order to deliver the version of "self" that is most useful in a given situation, with a particular person, and for a specific purpose. Identity is a valuable tool of communication. Use it with purpose and skill.

■

Lesson 4
Find, Seize, or Steal Some Privacy

> "To tell the truth, I cared not at all for hunting, but I passionately loved horseback riding. The more violent the exercise, the better I liked it, so that if a horse broke loose, I chased after it and brought it back. Also during this time, I always had a book in my pocket; if I had a moment to myself, I used it to read."
>
> ~*Memoirs*, 1759–1794

Empress Elizabeth saw to it that Catherine was always monitored by some spy or other. In her *Memoirs,* Catherine called such courtiers "Arguses"–Argus being the giant creature from Greek mythology who possessed a hundred eyes. In her struggle to eke out privacy whenever and however she could, Catherine joined hunting parties–less to hunt than to ride. She liked nothing better than chasing after runaway horses, an activity that brought not only the "violent" exercise she craved, but also time away from the other members of the party. She even went so far as to equip herself with a convenient book, so that she might capture a few fugitive moments for quiet reading out-of-doors when she was at a distance from the others.

The greater your leadership responsibility, the less time you have to call your own. It is nevertheless critically important to find, borrow, steal, or invent occasions to enjoy a degree of privacy. Not only is the emotional break necessary; time alone will give you a fresh perspective on your organization. Never feel guilty about elevating the need for privacy to a high priority—not only for yourself, but for the continued advancement of your enterprise.

■

Lesson 5

Find Motivation in Criticism

> "I do not know whether as a child I was really ugly, but I remember well that I was often told that I was and that I must therefore strive to show inward virtues and intelligence. Up to the age of fourteen or fifteen, I was firmly convinced of my ugliness and was therefore more concerned with acquiring inward accomplishments and was less mindful of my outward appearance."
>
> ~*Memoirs*, 1759–1794

Sophie Friederike Auguste of Anhalt-Zerbst would grow into an empress widely admired for her beauty, but as a girl she not only thought of herself as ugly, she was told by her mother and others that she was ugly and had, therefore, better work on developing her "inward virtues and intelligence."

There is no evidence that feeling ugly had a depressing effect on young Sophie. Even having those feelings corroborated by adults did not seem to discourage the girl. Instead, she took the advice at face value and concentrated on improving her intellect and other intangible qualities. She read voraciously and pursued her education avidly.

Despite being the victim of what we would now consider emotional abuse, the future Catherine II was reportedly a lively, happy child. She seems to have had no great difficulty turning her own negative self-image, reinforced by others, into a powerful means of self-motivation that served her well in focusing important early mental and emotional efforts.

Sophie was clearly an exceptional individual. No modern child psychologist would recommend reinforced self-loathing as a motivational tool. For many children, such attempts at "motivation" would produce depression or worse, but history is not devoid of accomplished individuals who used their emotional or circumstantial hardship as a springboard for success. We learn from the example of this empress-in-the-making that disappointment in one facet of life can propel a person to overcompensate for perceived deficiencies or hard luck in another facet. In Sophie's case, the perception that her looks were not sufficient to attract a worthy suitor motivated her to develop other attractive qualities that eventually made her one of the most admired monarchs in history.

If you encounter an obstacle, reconfigure it as an opportunity. Perceived defects, gaps, or deficiencies are motives for developing valuable workarounds, alternatives, skills, and innovative talents. Thus, criticism, disappointment, and low self-image can paradoxically guide you to identify and nurture your greatest strengths.

Lesson 6
Master Your Emotions

> "I told myself that life with this man [Grand Duke Peter] would certainly be very unhappy if I allowed myself tender feelings that were so ill repaid, and that to die of jealousy was of no benefit to anyone."
>
> ~*Memoirs*, 1759–1794

Catherine entered into marriage with Grand Duke Peter in the full knowledge that he did not love her. Her objective in marrying him was to gain access to power, to find a path to the throne. To achieve this, she "endeavored to conquer [her] pride, to not be jealous at all of a man who did not love me." She discovered, however, that the "only way not to be jealous was to not love him." Her natural inclination was to love a husband, but it was also true that "for this I would have needed a husband endowed with common sense, and this man did not have any."

Modern psychology tells us that it is a grave and destructive mistake to attempt to deny your emotions or even to attempt to "master" them. Perhaps, then, Catherine's success—at surviving, at gaining power, at governing—was less in her ability to conquer her emotions than in her refusal to be victimized by them. She understood love as an investment of emotion in another person. If that person failed to repay her investment, she was determined to stop squandering her emotional capital. Love, as she saw it, had to be an equitable exchange. To accept anything less than this was to agree to victimhood—and that, no leader could afford to do.

■

Lesson 7
Make Friends

> "I treated everyone as best I could and made it my task to earn the friendship or at least to lessen the enmity of those whom I suspected of being evilly disposed toward me."
>
> ~ *Memoirs*, 1759–1794

Some leaders believe that it is better to be respected–or even feared–than loved. Catherine wanted to be loved. Failing that, she wanted to make friends. And failing even this, she wanted to avoid making enemies. Her objective was to create an environment in which people felt they had a stake in her well-being. To this end, she endeavored to show "no preference for any side"–she minded her own business and "always had a serene air, much kindness, attentiveness, and politeness for everyone." In this way, she believed, she earned "from day to day . . . the affections of the public."

The most sustainable and productive relationships are those built on some degree of affection and empathy. We value those most highly for whom we have fellow feeling and understanding. Our interest in them impels us to promote their well-being and success. Friendship is not incompatible with business. On the contrary, it both facilitates and sustains business as the equitable exchange of value for value.

■

Lesson 8
Develop and Defend What Endures

"Only character endures."

~ *Memoirs*, 1759–1794

Alexander Shuvalov, a member of Empress Elizabeth's inner circle and, early on, among Catherine's most treacherous adversaries, criticized her for wearing a kind of ornamental lace and ribbon the empress had forbidden. As usual, Catherine responded by standing her ground. She told Shuvalov that she "never wore anything that displeased Her Majesty," and then continued in a broader context, telling "him that merit was not a matter of beauty, clothes, or ornament; for when one has faded, the others become ridiculous, and only character endures." At this, Catherine recorded in her *Memoirs,* Shuvalov's face began to twitch, and he left.

Catherine paid scrupulously close attention to what she wore. She wanted to be attractive, but she knew enough to avoid outshining or even appearing to outshine the Empress Elizabeth, especially at court events. Yet, while surfaces were highly important to her, she believed that "character" ultimately trumped appearance. Thus, she devoted herself to building her personal brand, associating it with integrity, loyalty, and courage.

> ***Character* is an** old-fashioned word. In a business context, you may be more comfortable with the phrase "personal brand." Either way, at stake is a reputation for integrity, loyalty, and courage. Character—a positive personal brand—is created, developed, and protected through the actions you take. Each transaction either builds it or destroys it. Build it.

■

Lesson 9
Recognize Your Rubicon

> "I saw that I had a choice among three equally dangerous paths . . ."
>
> ~*Memoirs*, 1759–1794

During the era of the Roman Republic, the small river Rubicon was the boundary between the Roman province of Cisalpine Gaul and Italy proper. As governor of Cisalpine Gaul, Julius Caesar was also the commander of the Roman army within this province. By law, he was barred from crossing the Rubicon and entering Italy at the head of his troops. Believing, however, that the Roman Republic was bound for ruin under Pompey the Great, and seeing his own future leadership–even his life–in jeopardy, Caesar boldly led one of his legions across the forbidden river on January 10, 49 BCE. His purpose was to force a civil war that would decide the fate of Rome, and his own, once and for all. In reference to Caesar's act, the phrase "to cross the Rubicon" has come to signify any decisive choice from which there is no return and for which there is no undoing.

After her son, Paul, was born on September 20, 1754, Catherine's husband publicly declared, "God knows where my wife gets her pregnancies. I really do not know if this child is mine and if I ought to recognize it."

When she was informed of this remark, Catherine was "alarmed" and "angered." In fact, the child was quite possibly the offspring of an affair with one of her favorites, Sergei Saltykov; nevertheless, Catherine refused to respond either with shame, evasion, fear, or defensiveness. Instead, she took the offensive. To those who conveyed Peter's remark to her, she shot back: "You are all impudent fools. Make him swear that he has never slept with his wife and tell him that if he makes this oath, you will go immediately to share it with [Secret Police head] Alexander Shuvalov and the grand inquisitor of the empire."

It was a bold move. Catherine called Peter's bluff, gambling that he would hardly make an official proclamation of either his own serial infidelity or his inability to perform sexually, which also implied an inability to do his imperial duty by siring an heir to the throne. Catherine also knew, however, that had Peter made the accusation official, she might well have faced exile or even execution.

What moved her to cross this particular Rubicon?

To her, the grand duke's remark came as an epiphany. She saw, "from that moment," that she "had a choice among three equally dangerous paths": She could maintain the status quo, sharing "the Grand Duke's fortune, whatever it might be"; she could "be exposed constantly to everything it might please [Peter] to devise for or against [her]"; or she could "take a path independent of all events." Having laid out these three paths, she then saw the situation more clearly, calling it "a question of perishing with him, or by him, or saving myself, my children, and perhaps the state from the disaster that all this Prince's moral and physical faculties promised." Dangerous though it was, the third path–independence–seemed to Catherine "the surest."

Having crossed her Rubicon, Catherine laid out her immediate course of action. She would, she decided, continue to advise Peter as best she could, always trying to "open his eyes to his true interests every time the occasion would present itself." As for the rest of the time, she resolved to "shut [herself] up in a very dull silence," even as she cultivated her "reputation with the public so that it would see in me the savior of the commonweal if the occasion arose." In short, the strategy was survival until a time when she could emerge to supplant Peter and, with public acclamation, ascend the throne.

Look with fresh eyes at the landscape of the status quo, and you may recognize your Rubicon flowing through it. When you do, you will need to weigh the wisdom of whether or not to make the crossing—and, equally important, what course to take after you cross. Few who attain success in any high-stakes enterprise are lifted to power by the status quo. Almost all cross a Rubicon, often more than once. There is rarely reward without risk, and, often, the safest-seeming course—namely, inaction—is the riskiest of all.

■

Lesson 10

Go for Broke

> "I am resolved . . . to perish or reign."
>
> ~Catherine, letter to Sir Charles Hanbury Williams, the British diplomat who introduced her to Stanisław Poniatowski, whom she eventually made king of Poland, October 1756

Once Catherine decided that she must find a way, not only to survive as the consort of the treacherous grand duke Peter, but ultimately to rise above him and rule Russia in her own name, she framed her resolution in do-or-die terms. For her, this was the ultimate expression of determination and not just a figure of speech. Increasingly, she focused on the throne, accumulated the friendship of more and more influential figures in the Russian court, cultivated the loyalty of the army, and when Czar Peter III provided provocation–by giving Russian territory to Prussia–she stood ready to fill the vacuum created by leading a lightning coup against her estranged husband.

Faced with a do-or-die situation, Catherine took a commensurate do-or-die approach. She did not act with stealth, gradually and covertly undermining Peter's reign. Rather, she seized the developing situation, made an instant and firm decision to assume leadership of the rapidly forming coup d'état, and spectacularly brought it all into the public sunshine. Catherine went for broke, not merely accepting the support of troops loyal to her, but actually leading them astride a white charger, arrayed in a grandly improvised uniform of an elite grenadier officer. Thus, she made a spectacle of the overthrow of Peter III and left no doubt as to the authorship of that spectacle. Having seized the throne, she embraced the people, including *them* in her triumph, giving *them* a stake in her ascension, making *them* the true victors in the battle she had led.

The do-or-die, go-for-broke approach is not widely regarded as a viable business model. Most business strategists counsel the importance of creating a clear path of retreat and a solid Plan B. Nevertheless, history provides many examples of great leaders who took the all-or-nothing approach at a critical juncture, finding in it just the stimulus their passion demanded. Caesar risked all in crossing the Rubicon, and the Spanish conquistador Hernán Cortés, on reaching the New World, drilled holes in the hulls of his ships so that there would be no easy turning back. Likewise, despite years of cultivating allies and knowledge of her adopted country, it wasn't until Catherine recognized that she was in a position to "do or die" that she willfully overthrew her inept, deceitful husband—in dramatic and inclusive fashion.

■

The Self-Made Monarch

CATHARINE II. ALEXIEVNA. EMPRESS OF RUSSIA. REIGNED XXXV YEARS.

Lesson 11

Make—and Keep—Promises to Yourself

> "I promised this to myself, and when I have promised myself something I cannot recall ever having failed to do it."
>
> ~*Memoirs*, 1759–1794

The Swedish diplomat Count Henning Gyllenborg, who had first met Sophie in Hamburg and had been greatly impressed with her, encountered the princess again–this time in Elizabeth's court. Having told her in Hamburg that she "had a very philosophical turn of mind," he now asked her in St. Petersburg how her "philosophy was faring in the whirlwind in which [she] had landed." He expressed concern "that a philosopher of fifteen could not yet know herself" and warned her that she "was surrounded by so many pitfalls that it was greatly to be feared that [she] would stumble." Accordingly, he advised her to "nourish" her "soul" with "the best readings possible" and recommended *Plutarch, an English life of Cicero*, and Montesquieu's *The Cause of the Grandeur and Decline of the Roman Republic*. Catherine immediately sent for these books, which were difficult to find in St. Petersburg at that time. Next, she told Gyllenborg that she was "going to compose my portrait such as I knew myself so that he could see whether or not I knew myself."

A short time after this, Catherine handed Count Gyllenborg "Portrait of the Philosopher at Age Fifteen." The autobiographical essay–now lost–greatly impressed the diplomat. After reading it, he returned the manuscript to her, joining "to it a dozen pages of reflections concerning me, in which he attempted to fortify in me spiritual strength and firm will as well as other qualities of heart and mind."

Catherine was deeply impressed and moved by Gyllenborg's interest.

"I read and reread his words a number of times," she wrote in her *Memoirs*. "I absorbed them and resolved quite seriously to follow his advice."

Her resolution was serious. It was a promise she made to herself, "and when I have promised myself something I cannot recall ever having failed to do it." She recorded in her *Memoirs* that what Gyllenborg had written "greatly aided in forming and fortifying the mettle of my mind and my soul."

We all make decisions every day. For the most important of these decisions, cultivate the habit of making promises to yourself—and keep them. Integrity begins with being true to yourself, your intentions, and your plans.

■

Lesson 12

Make the Most of Your Time

> "Eighteen years of tedium and solitude led her to read many books."
>
> ~Catherine II, "Epitaph," composed in 1778

As her *Memoirs* make vividly clear, Catherine's early years in the Russian court of the Empress Elizabeth were dreary and confining. As far as Elizabeth was concerned, Catherine's role in the Russian government was simple and strictly limited: Marry Elizabeth's nephew, Peter Ulrich, and produce with him a viable heir to the throne.

But Catherine–even as a young girl named Sophie–refused to be defined by anyone. With her scope, prospects, and even her physical movements severely confined by Empress Elizabeth, she immersed herself in the wider world through reading. The books she loved were not frivolous escapist works, but rather philosophical and historical tomes–books intended not merely to develop the mind, but to open windows on the world. Essentially confined to the isolated and provincial court of Elizabeth, Catherine would have understood what the nineteenth-century American poet Emily Dickinson meant when she wrote, "There is no frigate like a book." Nearly two decades of "tedium and solitude" provided ample space for Catherine the Great to enlarge her vision and shape her outlook in preparation for a mature life of rule.

You *can* transform "tedium and solitude" into enlightenment and engagement. Fill every empty hour with useful information, analysis, and contemplation.

■

Lesson 13

Seek the Causes

> "I began to . . . seek the causes that really underlay and truly shaped the different interests in the affairs that I observed."
>
> ~*Memoirs*, 1759–1794

Catherine was frequently left alone, in isolation, with many empty hours to fill. Most of them she filled with reading, which, early on, included two works that impressed her profoundly. One was *The Spirit of Laws,* published in 1748 by Charles de Secondat, Baron de Montesquieu. The product of some two decades of reading and research, this seminal political treatise called for the establishment of government based on civil liberties and a harmony between political institutions and the social and geographical realities of the community. Among other things, Montesquieu passionately advocated constitutional government and an end to slavery. In short, *The Spirit of Laws* championed government as an expression and elaboration of natural law and self-evident justice. Montesquieu argued that an organic government could not consist simply in the imposition of arbitrary authority on people. Instead, it had to be an institution that developed upward from those it governed.

While Catherine was impressed by the specifics of Montesquieu's theories, of greater interest to her was his having written not about the specific *conduct* of government, but about the broad *nature* of government. That is, he had explored the principles and drives that underlie the formation of government. It was for a similar reason that Catherine was captivated by another book during this period, the *Annals* of the Roman historian Tacitus. A key source for Roman history even today, *Annals* is no mere chronicle, but rather an exploration of the principles of government. Tacitus explores both the advantages and liabilities of government under the caesars, tempering the aspirations of idealism with the darker realities of tyranny. As with Montesquieu, Tacitus gets beneath the surface he documents so thoroughly.

Inspired by her early reading years before she ascended the Russian imperial throne, Catherine nurtured a predilection for discovering sources and root causes. Her rule would be guided by profound principle–perhaps the first time Russia had been so governed.

To the degree that you can discover and affect sources, motives, and causes, you multiply both the scope and the efficiency of your leadership. Seek roots, discover causes. As a building's solid foundation is critical to its strength, majesty, and endurance, so will a solid foundation of relevant knowledge contribute critically to the success of any enterprise.

Lesson 14
Choose a Hero or Two

> "I had read the life of Henry IV . . ."
>
> ~*Memoirs*, 1759–1794

Determined to educate herself, Catherine focused on history, the philosophy of government, and the biography of notable leaders. The historical figure who become her particular favorite–a personal hero, really–was Henry IV of France. Born in 1553, he reigned in Navarre beginning in 1572, and he ruled France from 1589 until his assassination by the Catholic fanatic François Ravaillac on May 14, 1610.

What did Catherine see in Henry? She does not specify in her *Memoirs* the reasons for her attraction to him, but they are not difficult to surmise. First, like her, he was a religious convert–from Catholicism to Protestantism, and then, for reasons of government, back to Catholicism. In this latter conversion, he demonstrated what Catherine must have regarded as a wise pragmatism, renouncing his Calvinist faith (it is said) by remarking, "*Paris vaut bien une messe*" ("Paris is well worth a Mass"), as if to suggest that the only *significant* difference between Protestantism and Catholicism was the fact that Catholics have Mass and Protestants don't. Rather than relinquish his reign over Catholic France, he would adopt the nation's prevailing religion. At the same time, however, Henry refused to perpetuate Catholic persecution of the Huguenots, France's Protestants. By promulgating the Edict of Nantes, he proclaimed religious toleration and thereby ended the kingdom's long, religiously based civil war. One of France's most popular monarchs, Henry IV was deeply concerned about the welfare of his subjects.

Pragmatic but principled, a leader who wanted to be remembered for his service to his people, Henry IV may well have been among Catherine's consciously chosen models for rule.

You are not the first person to manage a department, lead a team, or build a business. Look to history—of the world, of your industry, of your company—for successful leaders on whom to model your own reign. Find heroes and emulate them.

■

Lesson 15
A Liar Is a Liar

> "A liar is a liar, whatever his reasons for lying, and that fearing that this gentleman would involve me in his lies, I would speak to him no more. I kept my word; I spoke to him no more."
>
> ~ *Memoirs*, 1759–1794

An Italian diplomat, Count Santi, told a minor lie about Catherine–a lie that made it seem as if Catherine were publicly criticizing the behavior of the empress–to one of the duchess's court rivals, who in turn reported it to Elizabeth. Catherine stood up for herself, denied Santi's tale, and was cleared of wrongdoing. Nevertheless, when Santi tried to apologize to Catherine, explaining that he had been "forced" to lie, she refused to speak with him or even to acknowledge him in any way.

Questioned later about her treatment of Santi, she explained that his reason for lying did not matter to her. He was a liar, and because it was dangerous to be associated in any way with a liar, she resolved never to speak to him again.

Your credibility is coin of the realm. Speak and act with integrity and honesty, and you will do much to protect your credibility. What others do and say is, however, beyond your control. Especially dangerous are those who prove themselves unworthy of credibility. To associate with a known liar is to invite infection by proximity. Steer clear of those who demonstrate a lack of integrity. You cannot afford to risk contaminating your reputation.

■

Lesson 16

Embellish Reality

> "The Empress complimented me . . . . She told me that the letters that I had written in Russian to her in [her country residence in] Shotilova had brought her great pleasure (in truth, they were composed by [the Russian tutor] Monsieur Adadurov, but I had copied them in my hand) and that she knew I was studying hard to learn the language of the country."
>
> ~ *Memoirs*, 1759–1794

Eager to make a favorable impression on Empress Elizabeth–and especially to demonstrate her determination to remake herself into a good Russian–Catherine labored in earnest to master the language. While her effort was genuine, she was not above cheating in order to create the strongest possible impression. When the Empress Elizabeth was traveling away from court, Catherine had her Russian tutor write letters to her, which the young grand duchess copied in her own hand and sent off. It is not absolutely clear whether or not Elizabeth was wise to the deception. If she was, she nevertheless appreciated the intention of the charade and understood that Catherine "was studying hard to learn the language."

Catherine clearly understood the importance of creating complete satisfaction in her "customer," the empress of Russia. To this end, she embellished the reality of her sincerity—the determined effort she made to learn the Russian language—with the illusion of achievement beyond the level she had actually reached. In other words, she cheated.

Catherine spurned contact with Count Santi because she had caught him in a lie (Lesson 15), yet she herself was willing to stretch the truth. As a leader, the question you have to answer is how far to go in stage-managing the environment in which you and the members of your organization operate. Catherine decided that she could use all the help she could get. The key difference between her deception and Count Santi's was that, whereas his untruth was potentially injurious to her reputation at court, hers caused no harm to anyone. To what degree is carefully crafted illusion acceptable and even desirable in creating the "right feelings" among the members of your enterprise?

■

Lesson 17
Understand the Syllogism of Fortune

> "Fortune is not as blind as people imagine."
>
> ~ *Memoirs*, 1759–1794

Catherine the Great had at least one thing in common with Branch Rickey, the general manager of the Brooklyn Dodgers who, among other laudable achievements, racially integrated professional baseball by recruiting the great Jackie Robinson for his team in 1947. Rickey once famously declared, "Luck is the residue of design." Nearly two hundred years earlier, about as far away from Brooklyn as it is possible to be on planet Earth, Catherine the Great wrote that fortune was "not as blind as people imagine," but was "often the result of a long series of precise and well-chosen steps that precede events and are not perceived by the common herd." Fortune, she wrote, "is also more specifically the result of qualities, of character, and of individual conduct." To render these assertions "more concrete," she put them in the form of a syllogism: "Qualities and character will be the major premise," she wrote, "Conduct, the minor," and "Fortune or misfortune, the conclusion."

If you happen to be fuzzy on the structure of a categorical syllogism, recall this classic example:

Major premise: All humans are mortal.

Minor premise: All Greeks are human.

Conclusion: All Greeks are mortal.

Now, compare it to Catherine's syllogism:

Major premise: Qualities and character determine one's conduct.

Minor premise: Conduct determines one's fortune.

Conclusion: Quality and character determine one's fortune.

Add the "two striking examples" Catherine supplies: Herself and the husband, Peter III, whom she overthrew. The implied invitation is for you to insert these particulars into the syllogism:

Major premise: Catherine II's superior qualities and character produced admirable conduct.

Minor premise: Catherine II's admirable conduct led to good fortune.

Conclusion: Catherine II's superior qualities and character allowed her to enjoy good fortune.

Conversely:
Major premise: Peter III's inferior qualities and character produced disgraceful conduct.
Minor premise: Peter III's disgraceful conduct led to ill fortune.
Conclusion: Peter III's inferior qualities and character drove him to suffer ill fortune.

Or, as Catherine wrote to her friend and adviser, the German-born French author Friedrich Melchior, baron von Grimm (1723–1807), "The good fortune and misfortune of each is in his character; this character lies in the principles that the person embraces; success resides in the soundness of the measures that he employs to arrive at his ends; if he wavers in his principles, if he errs in the measures that he adopts, his projects come to nothing."

The Greek philosopher Heraclitus (c. 535–475 BCE) wrote, "Character is destiny." Like him, Catherine believed that we largely make our own destiny, which is the outward expression in deeds and outcomes of our own good judgment and integrity—or lack thereof. Effort devoted to building your character and the collective character of your enterprise, including integrity and judgment, will pay off in good fortune.

■

Lesson 18
Position Yourself

> "I . . . told him . . . to . . . ask the Empress to put him in a position where he could learn about the Empire's affairs."
>
> ~Catherine's advice to Grand Duke Peter, recalled in *Memoirs*, 1759–1794

In line for the Russian throne, Catherine's husband had no desire to rule over Russia. "He felt," she wrote in her *Memoirs,* "that he had not been born for Russia, that he did not suit the Russians nor the Russians him . . ."

Catherine nevertheless counseled him to position himself for future rule. First, she urged him to "do his best to make himself loved by every Russian," and, second, she advised him to persuade Empress Elizabeth to literally position him for knowledge and authority by allowing him to attend key conferences, to sit on important councils, and to play a role in the empire's affairs. Catherine understood that you create your own opportunities and that the first step toward this is to get yourself in all the right places at the right time.

Of course, Catherine knew that her husband was unfit to rule, but she also knew that unless he ascended the throne, her own eventual ascension would be impossible. By positioning Peter, she positioned herself.

Remember the words of the Brooklyn Dodgers' Branch Rickey: "Luck is the residue of design." Catherine could have adopted the maxim as her own, as it explains her unlikely rise to power and to greatness. If you aspire to leadership, continually engineer your position within each organization you inhabit. Get yourself closer and closer to the sources and means of authority. Observe and understand the mechanics of responsibility, then set about acquiring it.

Lesson 19
Define Your Identity

> "These notes concerning Russian history were composed for youth at a time when books on so-called Russian history are being published in foreign languages, which should rather be called prejudiced works."
>
> ~Catherine, remarks on her *Notes Concerning Russian History* (1783–1784)

Catherine wrote her *Notes Concerning Russian History* ostensibly for the use of her own grandsons, but authorized its publication for the general reader as well. She had become keenly aware that Russian history was being co-opted by foreigners, whose work, she correctly believed, could be nothing other than prejudiced. Thus, she took steps to reclaim the Russian identity and to broadcast it to Russians and the rest of the world.

If you fail to identify yourself, others will identify you—and their version will rarely be to your advantage. Never lose control of your reputation and your brand.

■

Lesson 20
Beware the Empty Boast

> "It seems to me that it is still early to present this proposal [to award the new Empress the title 'Mother of the Fatherland'] because it will be interpreted by the public as boasting . . ."
>
> ~Catherine, September 1763, quoted in John T. Alexander, *Catherine the Great: Life and Legend*

Three times early in her reign, Catherine declined offers from the Russian Senate to proclaim her "Mother of the Fatherland." It was a great honor–an imitation of the ancient Roman custom of proclaiming a great consul or other hero *Patris Patriae,* "Father of His Country"–and Catherine sincerely appreciated it. But, believing it to be premature, she was genuinely fearful that the public would judge the title as hollow. Catherine carefully cultivated her identity–or, as modern public relations professionals call it, her "personal brand." While she was especially concerned to avoid strong negatives, such as being popularly identified as a usurper and faithless wife, she was almost equally anxious to avoid inflation that would cheapen her brand and cause people to question her integrity and true value. Few monarchs possessed Catherine's self-discipline, which was sufficiently strong to enable her to resist the tremendous ego gratification of accepting so lofty a title.

Empty self-aggrandizement is destructive to a leader's brand. Reject such ringing adjectives as "great," "innovative," and "brilliant," and instead embrace verbs and nouns—the parts of speech that describe your actual acts and achievements. Rely on these to establish, embellish, and develop your brand.

■

Lesson 21
Look the Part

> "Her air is commanding and full of dignity."
>
> ~Sir George Macartney, British diplomat, 1766

Catherine took great care to fashion herself into the physical embodiment of her vision of an empress of Russia. During ordinary working days, she dressed modestly but impeccably. On ceremonial occasions, her "dress," as British diplomat Sir George Macartney wrote, was "never gaudy, always rich and yet still more elegant than rich." She made her biggest impression with the diamonds she wore. "She has shewn infinite taste in the manner of setting them," Macartney wrote, "nothing being more advantageous to their lustre." For her, the diamond–simple yet costly and dazzling–was the perfect emblem of her majesty.

As Macartney noted, her air of command was not merely a matter of costume. "Her eye," he wrote, "might be called fierce and tyrannical, if not softened by the other features of her face. . . . I never saw in my life a person whose port, manner, and behavior answered so strongly to the idea I had formed to myself of her": the idea of the majestic ruler of a vast realm.

No one who studies what Catherine II achieved in Russia can accuse her of being shallow. Yet she clearly understood the importance of surface appearance. No leader can afford to ignore the importance of the physical image he or she projects. Design an affirmative, positive, self-respecting, thoroughly professional look. Exhibit it whenever you are on the job.

Superficial? We come to know and evaluate our surroundings through surfaces. Create the most impressive surface you can.

■

Lesson 22
Create Satisfaction

> "To Monsieur Baron Alexander Cherkasov, from whose body I pledge by my honor to extract at least one burst of laughter daily or else to argue with him from morning until evening because these two pleasures are the same for him, and I love to give pleasure to my friends."
>
> ~Dedication to a portion of Catherine's manuscript for *Memoirs*, 1759–1794

She was, by title, "autocrat" of Russia and the inheritor of a tradition of absolute rule that dates back to Ivan the Terrible, who reigned from 1533 to 1584. One would think that giving pleasure would not be high on Catherine's inventory of objectives, and yet it was. She was quite willing to make hard decisions–to promote the deserving and to demote the undeserving, to reward the loyal and to punish the disloyal–and yet she also decided that it was easier to rule if one was liked and admired than if merely respected and feared. To a significant degree, she saw the sustenance of authority as linked to her ability to create satisfaction. Legally empowered to compel obedience, she vastly preferred eliciting voluntary compliance. As if she herself were a business, Catherine sought to build her brand by inspiring loyalty among her "customers."

To her friend, the courtier Baron Cherkasov, she dedicated a portion of what was at the time the manuscript of her *Memoirs,* a work that evolved over a number of years. What she wrote was humorous, yet also revelatory. She pledged herself to make her friend laugh daily *or* to argue with him "because these two pleasures are the same for him." So eager was Catherine to please her friend that she did not insist on the obvious route to pleasure, laughter, but also promised to argue with Cherkasov because *he* found pleasure in argument, "and I love to give pleasure to my friends."

Catherine was determined not to focus on herself or on the common revelations of received wisdom, but rather on what her "customer" wanted. She was, in this sense, what some today call a "servant leader," dedicated to creating satisfaction among those she leads.

Loyalty is a great value, and, like other great values, it is not given freely, but always in exchange for value received. You have it within your power as a manager to deliver value to all of your stakeholders by creating satisfaction among them. Your ongoing leadership authority is proportional to the degree of satisfaction you consistently create.

■

Lesson 23

Adapt to All People

> "I can adapt myself to all people. I am like Alcibiades in Sparta and in Athens."
>
> ~Letter to Princess Dashkova, July 31, 1789

When she was a thirteen-year-old, accompanying her mother in Hamburg, Germany, Sophie met the Swedish diplomat Count Henning Gyllenborg. He recognized something special in the girl, chiding Johanna, her mother, for exhibiting impatience with her daughter.

"Madame," he said, "you do not know the child. I assure you she has more mind and character than you give her credit for. I beg you therefore to pay more attention to your daughter for she deserves it in every respect."

To Sophie, Gyllenborg recommended the reading of certain key books, the most important of which was Plutarch's *Lives of the*

Noble Greeks and Romans, a compendium of biographies of the great leaders of the classical world.

She read it, and it became her lifelong companion. One of the biographies that most attracted her during her maturity was that of Alcibiades (c. 450–404 BCE), the extraordinary Greek *strategos* ("general") of the Peloponnesian War, who was as famed for the ease with which he changed allegiance from Athens, to Sparta, to Persia, to Athens again as he was for his strategic and tactical military genius. In 1790, Catherine translated this biography, along with the life of Coriolanus, to Russian.

In comparing herself to Alcibiades, Catherine laid aside questions of loyalty and treason and focused exclusively on the phenomenal thoroughness with which Alcibiades adapted to contrasting sets of people. Clearly, she saw a parallel in her own thoroughgoing transition from German Lutheran princess to Russian Orthodox monarch–a woman freely hailed by her subjects as "mother" of Russia. She saw her great quality as the ability to identify wholly and selflessly with whatever people she was to lead and to serve. She did not let the circumstances of her birth dictate her identity and loyalty.

You must become one with—and one of—those you lead. Fail to identify with the people of your organization, and your vision, as well as your ability to manage, will be half-hearted and ultimately ineffective. Catherine the Great was a Russian neither by birth nor by upbringing, yet she transformed herself into one of the greatest Russians of all. This transformation drove her leadership.

■

Lesson 24
Disarm Your Enemies

> "There was neither a friend nor an enemy who had not taken away some bauble to remember me by . . ."
>
> ~ *Memoirs*, 1759–1794

One of the techniques young Catherine used to win support among the contentious and often treacherous courtiers of Empress Elizabeth was to stage a lavish entertainment–a party that cost some fifteen thousand rubles, when she had a yearly stipend of just thirty thousand–for those she perceived as her friends, neutrals, and–most important–her enemies. She was determined not to destroy her enemies, but to "disarm" them. The party culminated in the distribution of favors–carefully chosen gifts that moved her guests to say, "This was given to me by Her Imperial Highness, the Grand Duchess. She is kindness itself, she gave presents to everyone, she is charming, she looked at me affably with a laugh on her face."

The gifts, Catherine pointed out in her *Memoirs*, were not particularly expensive, but they were linked to the impression she had carefully sought to make through this party. They were tokens, souvenirs that spoke of a woman who "took pleasure in having us dance, eat, and promenade." She put herself across as someone who ensured that everyone had a place to sit and who "wanted us to see what there was to see." In short, the gifts were intended to remind all the guests that here was a young woman who "was joyful" and who wanted others to feel that joy with her.

By creating something that gave others good feelings associated with her, Catherine fashioned a beneficent reputation and image. She wrote, "On that day people discovered qualities in me that they had not known I possessed," and in this way, she "disarmed" her enemies.

Find or invent ways to please colleagues, subordinates, bosses, clients, and customers. Build your identity into a "brand" that consistently promises the benefit of high value and individual attention.

■

Lesson 25
Context Is Everything

> "At court balls that the public did not attend, I dressed as simply as I could, and so paid my respects to the Empress, who did not much like anyone to appear overdressed."
>
> ~*Memoirs*, 1759–1794

In public appearances, Catherine dressed in ways designed to make what she characterized as "a big impression." In this, she spared no expense. But in formal and official settings closed to the public, she took care never to outshine the Empress Elizabeth–her most important "customer," the woman with the power to raise her up or knock her down. Catherine was hardly a shrinking violet, and she was eager to make an impression. Nevertheless, she possessed the judgment and self-discipline to allow others to outshine her when she thought this necessary to advance her career. Context, for her, was everything.

There is no one look or single costume that dresses you for success. The physical impression you make is an important aspect of what military leaders call your "command presence," but the effect of that impression is interactive—it always relates to the context in which it is enacted. Sales professionals are often told to "dress a notch above" their customers. This is, in fact, a useful rule of thumb for building your own command presence. Your objective is neither to look too casual within the context of your work environment, nor too formal or ostentatious. Assess the prevailing look of your environment and tailor your look to appear just over its horizon. The ideal leadership impression projects you above the crowd, even as it connects you to those you lead—or aspire to lead.

■

Lesson 26
Understand the Economy of Effect

> "If the costume I wore attracted everyone's praise, I was sure never to wear it again, because I had a rule that if it had made a big impression once, it could only make a smaller one the next time."
>
> ~ *Memoirs*, 1759–1794

Catherine II was a hardworking, eminently practical monarch and manager. Nevertheless, she possessed a deep appreciation of the theater of leadership. For her, it was always critically important to make a big impression. She understood, however, that there was a most stringent economy involved in making a powerful effect. Passionately fond of ornate dress and extravagant jewelry, she took care never to dilute the effect of a regal appearance through familiarity. If she perceived that a costume created a compelling effect, she may have been tempted to wear it over and over again–but she never did. She held it as a rule of human behavior that novelty played a large part in creating a "big impression." For this reason, she never wore the same magnificent raiment more than once in public. Each new "big impression" required a new costume, regardless of cost.

> **Effective leadership benefits** from the judicious application of "theater" from time to time. Know when to invest in making a big impression, and be willing to make the investment, even if it seems extravagant. The decision to "go big" requires careful judgment and courage born of considerable self-confidence, but it can pay off. Over-the-top can be cost effective if it creates a powerfully positive effect. Just be aware, as Catherine was, that the big impression must be made the very first time it is attempted and, once made, cannot be repeated—at least not with the same visuals and script.

■

Lesson 27
Rebrand Your Enterprise

> "Russia is a European power."
>
> ~ *The Great Instruction, or Nakaz* (1767), opening statement

As the Enlightenment gave way to the Age of Reason in the mid eighteenth century, Russia appeared to the rest of Europe as an "Asiatic" throwback to an earlier, benighted, and even barbaric age. Indeed, the likes of England, France, Italy, Germany, and other Western European countries refused to accept Russia as "European" at all.

When Catherine took the throne in 1762, her empire was under intellectual and moral siege by those in the West. She understood that, thanks to the "Asiatic" despotism of her predecessors–including the "Westward-looking" Peter the Great–

the Russian *brand* was badly tarnished. The empress therefore set out to, not so much rehabilitate Russia as rebrand the nation altogether. In this project, she pursued five main tracks:

1. She sought to reform Russian government through her ambitious, widely translated, and extensively published statement of legal principles called *The Great Instruction* (*Nakaz*), which, she hoped, would transform the "medieval" and "barbaric" Russian system of law into a rational legal code sufficiently enlightened to serve as an example for all Europe.

2. She sought to continue the work Peter the Great had begun by opening Russia even more fully to the West. Where Peter had established St. Petersburg on the Baltic, Catherine acquired the Crimea and, with it, a great port on the Black Sea. Now Russia had water passages to Europe both at its northern and southern frontiers.

3. She consulted and corresponded with the great minds of Europe–especially the French *philosophes* Voltaire and Jean-Jacques Rousseau, as well as the great encyclopedist Denis Diderot–in a sincere effort to open Russia to the most advanced Western thought.

4. For herself and Russia, she purchased the libraries of both Diderot and Voltaire and, with Diderot's help and advice, acquired a vast collection of European paintings, including many masterpieces, which became the foundation of the collection now housed in the Hermitage in St. Petersburg.

5. She fashioned herself into what she thought of as an exemplary Enlightenment monarch who not only ruled in

> the light of reason, but wrote an impressive body of literature. Although Catherine is today best remembered as a memoirist, she also wrote more than two dozen plays and opera libretti, as well as pieces for Russian and European periodicals. She produced essays on politics, education, economics, linguistics, and Russian history. She even wrote the first Russian literature intended for children. The empress was fluent in her native German, of course, as well as both Russian and French. She published–often anonymously–in all of these languages.

Perhaps Catherine's most effective projection of herself into the world of Western Europe as a representative of Russia was via her voluminous correspondence with the most enlightened, intelligent, fashionable, and influential figures in England, Germany, and especially France. In well over a thousand surviving letters, she effectively participated in what the eighteenth century called "salon society," the literary-intellectual-social space in which the high culture of her day was created. Catherine and her correspondence served as a conduit through which Russia became increasingly integrated with Western Europe.

A brand is more than a label; it is an identity that embodies and conveys value to others. For this reason, a great brand is worth creating, cultivating, developing, defending, and, should the brand ever prove counterproductive, revising. The fully committed CEO or owner must take a role of hands-on leadership, ensuring that his or her public persona embodies, enhances, and broadcasts the most productive brand of the enterprise.

■

Lesson 28

Create Labels to Control Perception

> "A deserter and fugitive has been collecting . . . a troop of vagabonds like himself . . . and has had the insolence to arrogate to himself the name of the late emperor Peter III. . . . As we watch with indefatigable care over the tranquility of our faithful subjects . . . we have taken such measures to annihilate totally the ambitious designs of Pugachev and to exterminate a band of robbers who have been audacious enough to attack the small military detachments dispersed about these countries, and to massacre the officers who have been taken prisoner."
>
> ~Catherine, manifesto condemning Pugachev, December 19, 1774

In 1774 and 1775, Catherine's reign was menaced by a popular rebellion headed by Yemelyan Pugachev, a former lieutenant of the Imperial Russian Army. Catherine responded not only militarily, but also rhetorically. She issued a manifesto, using labels designed to shape or reshape the popular perception of Pugachev and his followers.

To begin with, the manifesto labels Pugachev not as a former army officer or even as a rebel, but as a "*deserter and fugitive*"–in effect, a coward and criminal of the lowest possible character. Catherine avoids calling his followers a rebel band, let alone an army. Instead, they are "*a troop of vagabonds*"–and not just vagabonds, but "*vagabonds like himself.*"

Pugachev's avowed objective of setting up, in the name of Peter III, an alternative to Catherine's government, the empress calls "*insolence.*" His "*designs*" are "*ambitious*"–that is, his schemes are for the sake of his own advancement, not to advance the best interests of the country. What is the proper response to them? Catherine calls for "*total annihilation*" and the "*extermination*" of the lowly, parasitic "*band of robbers*", who have already been foolish enough to attack military detachments and "*massacre*" Russian officers.

Catherine's manifesto concerning Pugachev is not random name-calling, but rather a studied exercise in creating perception via labels. In so far as perception drives choices, creates loyalties, and motivates actions, perception *is* reality. Catherine knew enough to supply the critically needed labels for a reality that would keep her in the public's high regard. Control perception and you control reality.

■

Lesson 29
Recognize the Power of Success

> "The fact is that it is only since I have enjoyed good fortune that Europe finds me so clever. At forty, however, one scarcely improves in intelligence or looks, in the sight of the Lord."
>
> ~Catherine, letter to Voltaire, 1770

The greatest Russian victory in the Russo-Turkish War of 1768–1774 was the massive triumph of the Russian naval fleet over that of the Ottoman Empire in Çeşme Bay on July 5–7, 1770. Despite the loss of perhaps six hundred Russians, the outnumbered Russian fleet destroyed seventy-three Ottoman ships, including sixteen huge ships of the line, killing some eleven thousand Turkish sailors. For this and subsequent victories, all of Europe hailed Catherine. Voltaire himself called her "the avenger of Europe."

Without a doubt, Catherine reveled in the glory, but she never forgot that it was her "good fortune" that drew all the praise. In its absence, she would have been regarded as little more than another middle-aged monarch.

"Nothing succeeds like success," the old saying goes. Few sovereign rulers worked harder than Catherine the Great to prepare themselves to govern. She cultivated her mind over a long period, beginning when she was very young. Yet she also understood that her leadership would ultimately be measured not by her personal qualities, but by the results she achieved. In the eyes of the world, her value was proportionate to her success. That did not cause her to resent her achievements, but, rather, to elevate them even higher in importance and to make her hungry for more and greater success. She focused on consolidating the gains made in the 1768–1774 war, formally annexing the Crimea in 1783, and she continually pushed for greater recognition from Western Europe, mediating peace in the War of Bavarian Succession (1778–1779) and engineering the successive partitions of Poland, On the domestic front, she continually worked toward improving banking and finance and promoting a general cultural and intellectual awakening. Thus, Catherine II seems to have understood that, for all except one's closest relatives and loved ones, a leader's worth is directly proportionate to the successes achieved—and the failures suffered.

■

Lesson 30
Make Your Point Monumental

"Petro Primo Catharina Secunda MDCCLXXXII"

~Catherine's inscription on the base of her monument to Peter the Great

In 1766, Catherine, acting on the recommendation of Denis Diderot, commissioned the French sculptor Étienne-Maurice

Falconet to create a massive equestrian monument to Peter the Great in the Senate Square at St. Petersburg. Created entirely of bronze, the statue is twenty feet high–exclusive of its twenty-five-foot-high stone base, which, at some fifteen hundred tons, was fashioned from what is generally believed to be the largest stone ever moved by men without the aid of powered machinery.

Falconet began work on the monument in 1770, and casting began in 1775. The monument was finally completed in 1782, after twelve years (fourteen years, if you start the count from the year that excavation of the great pedestal "Thunder Stone" had begun).

The inscription on the base, which Catherine composed both in Latin and in Russian, translates as "To Peter the First, From Catherine the Second, 1782." Its meaning is dual, signifying that Catherine has dedicated the monument to Peter, whom she deeply admired, but also that Catherine felt justified in defining her reign as a continuation of Peter's. The empress remained keenly aware that she had ascended the throne by means of a coup d'état, and the bigger-than-life monument was clearly intended to symbolically underscore her legitimacy directly in the line of Peter the Great. She understood that no amount of verbal argument in defense of her right to rule could speak louder than this massive structure of bronze and stone–one of the great heroic sculptures in the world.

> **Let there be** no ambivalence or ambiguity about the major statements you make. Deliver them in the equivalent of bronze and stone. When you have a point to make, make it monumental.

■

Lesson 31
Learn from Misfortune

"Misfortune is a great teacher . . ."

~Catherine, concerning the prospects of the French counterrevolutionary Count of Artois, March 1793

From March 12 to March 15, 1793, Catherine II celebrated the Count of Artois and his entourage, who came to Russia as refugees from the French Revolution, which they had hoped to overthrow. Artois was widely thought of as a possible successor to King Louis XVI, who had recently been guillotined. When he prepared to leave Russia, Catherine presented the count with a gold sword, decorated with a diamond solitaire and bearing the inscription: "With God for the King." She believed he possessed "an excellent heart, a very quick understanding, [and] good sense," and she predicted–more out of hope than true belief, perhaps–that he would have ultimate success. "Misfortune is a great teacher," she remarked to Friedrich Melchior von Grimm, a frequent confidant, observing further that France's Henry IV, a personal hero of hers, "did not know any more than [the Count of Artois] does."

We all hope in our careers to encounter mentors and sponsors whom we will deeply admire and for whom we will feel deep affection. Some of us are fortunate enough to find them. Don't await their arrival. Instead, learn from all the teachers you encounter, whether their message is born of happiness or sadness, success or failure, achievement or catastrophe. Experience itself, regardless of content and outcome, is a valuable teacher, provided it is encountered by a ready student.

■

The Ambitious Woman

CATHARINE II. ALEXIEVNA. EMPRESS OF RUSSIA. REIGNED XXXV YEARS.

Lesson 32
Mine Your Core

> "My heart did not foresee great happiness; ambition alone sustained me. At the bottom of my soul I had something, I know not what, that never for a single moment let me doubt that sooner or later I would succeed in becoming the sovereign Empress of Russia in my own right."
>
> ~ *Memoirs*, 1759–1794

When Sophie arrived in Russia, she met her betrothed, a thoroughly repulsive young man with a long, drooping nose that hovered above a thickly protruding lower lip. Immature and sexually underdeveloped, he preferred playing with dolls and toy soldiers to enjoying the company of his fiancée. He often amused himself by torturing animals, ranging from his hunting dogs down to rats that infested the palace. The rats he would hang by miniature nooses, in mock martial execution, as a regiment of toy soldiers looked on. To make matters even worse, Peter consistently conspired with others in the palace to spy on Catherine and to fabricate damaging reports of her behavior, which were duly delivered to his aunt, the empress Elizabeth.

Little wonder that, in contemplation of married life with this man, Catherine's "heart did not foresee great happiness." Yet she did not allow herself to lose focus on her ultimate goal of becoming empress of Russia. It fed, she wrote, an inner "ambition" that "sustained" her throughout long periods of despair. Confronted by external disappointment and adversity, Catherine discovered an inner strength at the bottom of her soul, and, having discovered it, she mined it, digging deeply into herself. This was her treasure, she realized, and she would make the most of it.

The lesson common to the lives of most people who achieve greatness—or, at least, a success worthy of history's notice—is the faculty not merely of *overcoming* adversity but of *using* it. Most characteristically, these individuals use adversity to discover, realize, and activate some source of inner strength, drive, and guidance. Instead of retreating internally, as into a fortress, when confronted by adversity, they find an internal source of energy and direction. Then, armed and guided by it, they reemerge into the world, ready to do battle. Inner strength is best used to create the environment you need, the reality you want.

■

Lesson 33
Learn the Language

> "To make more rapid progress in Russian, I rose from my bed at night and, while everyone slept, memorized the lessons that [my Russian tutor] Adadurov gave me."
>
> ~*Memoirs*, 1759–1794

When Catherine II came to Russia as Sophie, a minor German princess, she spoke not a word of Russian. In fact, there was ample precedent, both in Russia and other countries, of royal transplants who never bothered to learn the language of the country over which they were expected to rule. But Catherine never thought of becoming anything other than thoroughly fluent in Russian. She believed it important to know the language of the court, the streets, and the fields. She believed that to the degree her Russian remained insufficient, she would be distanced from power, as well as from the high level of understanding that was required to govern her people effectively. Therefore, she made an extraordinary effort to learn the language, and her effort was extraordinarily successful.

Learn the language of your business. Understand all of the special terms and concepts, and become proficient in the applicable technologies. Learn the markets. Speak the language of colleagues as well as customers. Strive—or struggle, if necessary—toward complete fluency.

■

Lesson 34

Be Always Loyal

> "I told him that to please the Empress I would wear whatever hairstyle pleased her."
>
> ~*Memoirs*, 1759–1794

Young Catherine quickly learned how to navigate the treacherous landscape of the court of Empress Elizabeth. She prioritized her loyalties, setting above all others–including loyalty to her own mother–absolute fealty to the empress.

She made no secret of her unconditional allegiance to Elizabeth. When the Marquis de la Chétardie, the French ambassador and long a favorite of Elizabeth, betrayed the empress with critical remarks he made in letters to various correspondents, Elizabeth unceremoniously expelled the marquis from the royal court, as well as the Russian Empire. Before he left, the marquis praised Catherine for a new hairstyle she had adopted. Her reply was frank: "I told him that to please the Empress I would wear whatever hairstyle pleased her."

Clearly, her response hit home. The Marquis de la Chétardie "turned and went off in the other direction, and spoke to me no more."

If you hope to rise within an organization, identify the "customer" or "customers" you *must* satisfy. Never waver in your allegiance to those you identify as crucial to your status within an organization. This must be, unswervingly, your top priority.

■

Lesson 35

Consider the Strenuous Life

> "Here is the life I led . . . . I arose at three in the morning . . . . An old huntsman in my service was already waiting for me with some rifles . . ."
>
> ~*Memoirs*, 1759–1794

Young Catherine was a vigorous horsewoman. When Empress Elizabeth objected to her riding astride, like a man, she invented a saddle that was convertible, in the field, from a sidesaddle to a regular saddle. To please the empress, she would begin her rides in an appropriately "feminine" sidesaddle posture, and then, having reached a safe distance from the palace, convert her saddle so that she could ride like a man.

Whenever she could, Catherine would rise well before dawn, dress "from head to foot in a man's outfit," and go duck shooting. These expeditions were made partly on foot and partly in a skiff along a canal. "We often went out beyond the canal," she wrote, "and consequently were sometimes caught in rough weather on the open sea in the skiff." She loved it.

Had she lived in late nineteenth- and early twentieth-century America, Catherine the Great would doubtless have embraced the celebrated philosophy of Theodore Roosevelt, who extolled the virtues of living what he called "the strenuous life." He believed that a leader needed to cultivate physical as well as intellectual and moral strength, along with physical courage and a high degree of endurance. For this reason, Roosevelt actively sought adventure and hardship. Catherine took much the same approach. The harder she hiked, rode, sailed, or hunted, the stronger she felt. Thus, strenuous activities allowed her to build the confidence she needed to seize and wield power.

> **Choose to make** it very hard on yourself from time to time. Test yourself. Prove yourself *to* yourself. You need all the confidence you can create through the conquest of one concrete challenge after another.

■

Lesson 36
Keep Your Eye on the Prize

> "I saw clearly that he [Peter] would have left me without regret; as for me, seeing his feelings, I was more or less indifferent to him, but not to the crown of Russia."
>
> ~*Memoirs*, 1759–1794

History displays many tyrants and dictators far worse than the grand duke Peter, who would rule Russia for just six months as Peter III. But few historical figures have been more repulsive than Peter. Catherine's account of him is amply corroborated by others. Beyond doubt, he was pathologically immature (obsessively playing with dolls and soldiers as an adult), sexually underdeveloped (yet serially unfaithful), sadistic toward both human beings and animals, physically abusive to his wife, willfully ignorant, disloyal to his country, incompetent as a ruler, indifferent to the Russian people, and an alcoholic. Not surprisingly, when Peter repeatedly spurned Catherine, she became (she writes) "more or less indifferent to him."

Doubtless, this was an understatement. She was certainly very strongly motivated to leave him. Yet she did not, because she saw marriage to Peter as her pathway "to the crown of Russia."

It is easy to judge Catherine as the most determined kind of opportunist, willing to dissemble and to sacrifice basic affection, let alone romantic love, in order to obtain power.

So be it. However we may judge her, she was a determined leader who possessed sure self-knowledge, including a deep awareness of her goal. Having conceived a purpose in life, she pursued it to the exclusion of all else and was determined to endure revulsion, pain, rejection, and even heartbreak to achieve it.

We all need to assess and to weigh what objectives and values are important to us. For many, the sacrifices demanded by full dedication to a career are unacceptable, even unendurable. Today, many in our "success"-driven society find themselves torn between conflicting life paths, but the basic question of values is timeless. As Christ asked his disciples, "For what is a man profited, if he shall gain the whole world, and lose his own soul?" But if, like Catherine, you are determined to achieve a certain set of well-defined goals, you must, like her, be prepared to accept the sacrifices as well as the rewards. The choices involved can be painful, even ugly. That is a key lesson of the life Catherine II led.

■

Lesson 37

Make Yourself Indispensable

> "The Grand Duke had long been calling me Madame Resourceful, and however upset or sulky he was toward me, if he found himself in any distress, he ran as fast as he could, as was his habit, to my apartment to get my opinion . . ."
>
> ~*Memoirs*, 1759–1794

Although their marriage quickly degenerated into bickering and bitterness, with Grand Duke Peter both unfaithful and abusive, Catherine always behaved in ways that made her useful–even indispensable–to her husband. A weak and feckless man, he repeatedly turned to her for solutions to his many difficulties. Instead of withholding her counsel and aid, Catherine bestowed it freely and eagerly. To him, she became "Madame Resourceful," and, though he resented her, Peter found that he could not do without her.

The surest way to advance—or at the very least, to survive—within a challenging or outright hostile organization is to transform yourself into "Madame [or Mister] Resourceful." Take every opportunity to help. Make yourself knowledgeable in critical areas. Offer your counsel freely. Volunteer aid. Take ownership of problems, and then solve them. Brand yourself within the enterprise as the "go-to" resource. Resist the temptation to deny assistance, even to the manifestly underserving. Instead, make yourself indispensable to everyone, but especially to those with the power to advance you or to hold you back.

■

Lesson 38

Take Care of the Trifles

> "These are only trifles, but they must be taken care of . . ."
>
> ~Grand Duke Peter's secretary, quoted in *Memoirs*, 1759–1794

One morning, the grand duke Peter barged into Catherine's room. His secretary, a man named Zeitz, was running after him, a paper in hand.

"Take a look at this devil of a man," Peter implored his wife. "I drank too much yesterday. I am still completely hungover today, and here he is bringing me a sheet of paper and it is only the accounts register he wants me to finish. He even follows me into your room."

Exasperated, Zeitz told Catherine that everything he had on the paper in question was "a simple matter of yes or no." All he needed was fifteen minutes of the grand duke's time and attention.

Catherine offered to help, assuring her husband that perhaps he would finish sooner than he thought. Taking his cue, Zeitz began reading aloud, and Catherine herself "said yes or no." Instead of being upset at her usurping his authority, the grand duke smiled. The task quickly completed, thanks to Catherine, Zeitz admonished Peter: "You see, my lord, if you consented twice a week to do this, your affairs would not come to a halt. These are only trifles, but they must be taken care of, and the grand duchess has finished with six yes's and as many no's, more or less."

> **The details of management**—the "trifles"—are easy to put off. Do so, however, and they take on a cumulatively daunting importance that may stop you cold. Create routines to dispatch the details. Cultivate the discipline necessary to adhere to the routines you establish. This is not the fuel of leadership, but rather the lubricant—something just as necessary.

Lesson 39
Get It in Writing

> "I told him to give me a signed order concerning what I could or could not decide without his permission, which he did."
>
> ~*Memoirs*, 1759–1794

When Grand Duke Peter neglected to make routine decisions concerning the governance of his duchy of Holstein, Catherine volunteered to take over. Resolving to leave nothing subject to misunderstanding, however, she demanded from him a signed order specifying the boundaries of her authority. It was, in fact, a precise inventory of her powers in this particular sphere.

Movie mogul Samuel Goldwyn put it best: "A verbal contract isn't worth the paper it's written on." Appealing though it may be to your leadership style, avoid informal "verbal agreements." Put not only contracts, but also instructions, authorizations, observations, and evaluations in writing. The closer you can get to a numbered inventory or checklist, the better. Sign such documents, and require recipients to formally acknowledge (with signature and date) their receipt. Business, like all human interchange, offers many opportunities for dispute. Written documentation eliminates one key area of possible dispute: the memory of who said what, when.

■

Lesson 40

Do the Work

"I regularly get up at six A.M. . . ."

~Catherine, letter to Marie Thérèse Rodet Geoffrin, November 6, 1764

Some "absolute" rulers have looked upon their lot in life as a divinely decreed aspect of the proper order of the universe. Catherine the Great, however, understood that she had not been born into her role as empress of Russia, but rather had acquired it via a combination of marriage, her own exceptional qualities and skills, good fortune, courage, risk-taking, and the fact of her survival. She also believed that, in the turbulent world of Russian dynastic politics, her continuation on the throne depended entirely on the degree of success she achieved as a leader. She never took her authority for granted, and she was never complacent about maintaining it. Quite the contrary, she committed herself to the hard work of governing, governing well, and governing from a position informed by current events, cultural heritage, historical realities, and what we would today call the "best practices" of the most enlightened rulers of her day. Accordingly, she developed a rigorous work ethic and approached her position as a most demanding job.

"I regularly get up at six A.M.," she wrote. "I read and I write all alone until eight; then someone comes to read the news to me, those who have to speak to me come in one by one, one after the other, which can take until eleven or later, and then I dress." On Sundays and feast days, this routine was followed by attendance at mass. On other days, Catherine would retreat to her "antechamber, where a crowd of people usually awaits me, and after a half- or three-quarter-hour conversation, I sit down to lunch . . . and bring my papers." These she would read and work on until 5:30.

Commit yourself to the hard work of leadership. Identify the necessary tasks and introduce into your workday as much rigorous routine as possible. Do not await the arrival of inspiration. No matter how officially exalted, a leader is first and foremost a worker.

■

Lesson 41

Encourage a Culture of Conversation

> "My disposition was naturally so accommodating that no one was ever with me a quarter of an hour without falling comfortably into conversation, chatting with me as if they had known me for a long time."
>
> ~*Memoirs*, 1759–1794

Traditionally, "business people" have denigrated conversation as small talk, verbiage that takes time away from *real business*, which they define as discourse about deals, transactions, prices, discounts, products–you name it: anything that leads obviously and directly to the bottom line.

No one was busier than Catherine the Great. Not only did she lead one of the world's biggest empires, but she led it hands-on, delegating as few of the details as she possibly could. And yet she always made time for conversation, building it into her daily schedule. She thought of it specifically as "chatting," not as holding a political or philosophical debate or analyzing a report. *Small talk* played a big role in the court and the daily life of Empress Catherine II.

To fall "comfortably into conversation" with someone, to chat with him or her as if you have known him or her your whole life, is to open up and express yourself with easy honesty. For anyone in charge of a large, complex organization, frank, unguarded conversation is a source of tremendously useful information and insight. Catherine cultivated and mined such sources, which she valued highly. She also understood that she had to treat conversation as conversation–not as "gotcha gossip." She never used her chatting as a way of spying and ferreting out disloyalty or criticism. Rather, she regarded it as a means of informally taking the pulse of her court and her country. No one was ever punished for what they said to her. Had they been, Catherine knew, no one would want to "chat" with her again, and she would have lost access to an extraordinary channel of valuable, uncensored insight.

Chat. Encourage an office culture of conversation and "small talk." At the very least, such a climate creates bonds among the members your organization, who come to regard each other not merely as coworkers and colleagues, but as fully rounded human beings. Beyond this, conversation quickly becomes a key source of insight into the day-to-day operation of the organization. It is a monitor on the vital signs of the enterprise—the spirit, attitude, and morale of the place.

■

Lesson 42

Give Yourself Credit

> "I admit that when I despaired of succeeding on the first point, I redoubled my care to fulfill the last two, I thought I succeeded more than once on the second, and I succeeded on the third point to the fullest extent and without any reservations at any

time, and therefore I believed that I had attained my goal sufficiently."

~*Memoirs*, 1759–1794

While Catherine endured the difficulties of negotiating life in the Russian court during the reign of Empress Elizabeth, she believed she had three main jobs. The first was to please her husband, Grand Duke Peter; the second was to please Elizabeth; and the third was to please the nation. Catherine came to the realistic conclusion that she could never succeed at the first job and could only occasionally achieve success with the second. At the third job, however, she gave herself credit for being successful and took great satisfaction in this belief.

Acknowledge your failures, but also give yourself unstinting credit for your successes. Patting yourself on the back now and then will instill in you the confidence and the endurance to continue fighting and winning every battle that stands in the way of every great achievement.

■

Lesson 43

Value Your Portable Skills

"In whatever situation it should please Providence to place me, I would never find myself without those resources that intelligence and talent give to each according to his natural abilities, and I felt the courage to rise and fall without my heart and my soul feeling wither pride or vanity or . . . shame or humiliation."

~*Memoirs*, 1759–1794

Catherine was well aware of what was at stake, given her precarious position in the court of Empress Elizabeth. She could lose everything at any time–royal position, children, fortune, even her life–or she could gain the throne of imperial Russia. Yet she refused to invest her ultimate value–her identity–in her role and fate at court. She separated the values, abilities, and resources that formed her core from the benefits she received as a Russian royal. In modern terms, she never confounded her *self* with her *job*.

Very often, what separates a successful résumé from one that fails to get the job is the applicant's ability to offer a potential employer, not just a record of experience compiled in the employ of another, but a valuable set of what career counselors like to call "portable skills." These are the skills, qualifications, and competencies that travel with you and are not attached to a particular position. You may put them at the disposal of one employer after another, but they remain yours and represent your value in *any* position you may occupy.

To brand yourself as a leader, value your portable skills and present these, first and foremost, to anyone with whom you propose to work. Experience is history. Important though it is, history is never as valuable as the promise of a great future. That promise is represented by the dynamic skills, talents, and attitudes you carry with you as your value proposition to bosses, colleagues, employees, and customers.

■

Lesson 44
Focus and Refocus

> "She embraces too many objects at once; she likes to begin, regulate, and correct projects all in a moment."
> ~Lord Buckingham, British envoy to Russia, diary entry from 1763

To Lord Buckingham, the British envoy to the Russian imperial court, it appeared that the then-new empress, Catherine II, was trying to take on too much, too soon and all at one time. He seems not to have recognized what was most acutely apparent to her: Elizabeth and Peter III, her immediate predecessors, had left the empire in a most perilous state. Everything was going wrong at once–administratively, financially, militarily. Civil insurrection was a continual possibility. War with Prussia and the Ottoman Empire was always a threat. Reality simply would not wait, and Catherine resolved to address the most urgent needs simultaneously rather than serially.

One tool she had at her disposal in this multitasking effort was a mind that approached problems systematically, with rigorous rationality. Rather than viewing her methodical way of solving problems as the very faculty she needed to attend to so many matters at once, Buckingham was critical of it. He reported that her "foible is to be too systematic, and that may be the rock on which she may, perhaps, split."

Multitasking is not for everyone. For better or worse, however, modern management environments almost invariably demand that leaders juggle multiple operations while they solve multiple problems. The most effective managers do not actually multitask; they only appear to, as they address issues one after the other in quick succession, often breaking down large projects into smaller units they can focus on briefly before turning to other business. The idea is to avoid trying to concentrate on several matters at once by prioritizing, systematizing, and addressing bite-sized pieces of business in succession. Think not in terms of attention spread thinly over many projects, but rather of concentrated focus delivered in short bursts on particular aspects of one project after another.

■

Lesson 45

Rise Above It

> "Happiness and misery are in the heart and soul of everyone. If you feel misery, rise above it, and act so that your happiness does not depend on any event."
>
> ~ *Memoirs*, 1759–1794

Catherine preached as a leadership principle the necessity of total engagement with the enterprise one leads. In contrast to the vast majority of the Russian monarchs who had preceded her–most immediately, her own short-lived husband, Peter III and Empress Elizabeth–Catherine was a hands-on leader. Further, she was both a long-term visionary and a day-to-day manager. However, she always kept something in her innermost core entirely independent of her empire and the events associated with it. She refused to chain her happiness to anything outside of herself. Instead, she regarded it as her own exclusive asset and drew on it frequently for strength during the most challenging periods of her rule.

To lead effectively, you must identify wholeheartedly with your enterprise. However, it must never become your life. As important as the bond between you and your organization is—and that bond is necessary to create effectively engaged leadership—it is equally important to maintain an identity that is yours and yours alone. Your emotional well-being depends on this. The success as well as the future of your enterprise depends on your high morale and full emotional health. Even a dedicated "servant leader" must maintain a certain selfishness at the core.

■

Lesson 46
Know What You Don't Know

> "I confess I do not understand anything about great accounts and therefore I request you to note again, how much [money] do I have at my disposal, without halting any allocated expenditures."
>
> ~Catherine, to her secretary of state, Adam Olsufiev, 1767

Despite the extraordinary achievements of her reign, Catherine the Great proved no more successful than her predecessors at getting her arms around the finances of the Russian Empire. From 1724 to 1781, the Russian bureaucracy produced no comprehensive financial statement for the country. In contrast to both Empress Elizabeth and Peter III, however, Catherine earnestly tried to gain a full understanding of the empire's financial position, whereas her predecessors were quite content with their prevailing ignorance. Elizabeth coped with not knowing by maintaining a personal policy of extreme tightfistedness, while Peter III, in his brief reign, simply spent without any regard to the treasury balance.

Although Catherine failed to acquire a complete financial picture, she forged ahead with government as successfully as she did because she knew what she did not know. She was well aware of the gaps in her knowledge, which gave her sufficient margin to work around.

In modern business, there is no excuse for failing to acquire and maintain a comprehensive and accurate picture of the financial status of your enterprise. Nevertheless, at any point in time, business information will likely be incomplete. Not everything can be known—at least not with certainty. Many vitally important elements needed for informed business decisions may be missing at precisely the time when the decision must be made. Such is the nature of any dynamic enterprise. If you cannot know everything, you must at least know what you do not know. In this way, you can create contingencies, calculate risks, and maintain sufficient flexibility to take productive action rather than succumb to decision paralysis. If you know what you do not know, you can work around the holes, which means that you can move forward. Advancing with less than complete information is risky, but, in any competitive business environment, it is less risky than clinging to the illusion that the status quo is always safe. Know as much as you can, even if that means knowing that, from A to Z, you do not know C, F, H, and J. Calculate the rewards and risks of acting in the absence of this knowledge. Usually, you are better off taking action than waiting for someone else's action to overtake you.

■

Lesson 47
Make Contact, and Never Lose Touch

> "It is inconceivable with what address she mingles the ease of behavior with the dignity of her rank, with what facility she familiarizes herself with the meanest of her subjects, without losing a point of her authority . . ."
>
> ~Sir George Macartney, British diplomat, 1766

A common quandary among those who find themselves in leadership positions is how to present themselves as leaders without losing touch with those they lead. Catherine seems to have been a model leader insofar as she solved this problem, recognizing the need to appear regal and commanding without relinquishing what is often called the "common touch." In her case, this feat was the more remarkable because she was not even Russian by birth. Nevertheless, she embraced the country, its people, and its traditions as if they were her own. Once having embraced them, she never let go–not even after ascending the throne. In this ability, she called to the mind of many observers England's beloved "Good Queen Bess," Elizabeth I.

There is no doubt that Catherine II of Russia, like Elizabeth I of England, possessed a rare gift for leadership. She played the role of monarch to the hilt and with great success, yet she never allowed herself to lose contact "with the meanest of her subjects." Can any of us in leadership positions hope to achieve this delicate balance? The answer is: Each of us can try—and, in trying, we will achieve at least some measure of success. Begin by acknowledging that you and those who report to you all share a common stake in the success of your organization. Use this bond as a special reason to take an interest in all the members of your team. Learn to appreciate them as people, not just employees. You don't have to be a friend to everyone, but be friendly. You can set the workplace bar of performance high without sacrificing appreciation and empathy for team members as human beings. Begin by showing interest in those you work with. Work at it. Very soon, that interest will be absolutely genuine, and you will come across with at least some of the magic that Catherine the Great possessed.

■

Lesson 48

Undertake an "Immense Work"

"This is an immense work . . ."

~Catherine, letter to Marie Thérèse Rodet Geoffrin, 1765, on her project to codify Russian law

Beginning in February 1764, less than two years after she ascended the throne, Catherine began work on what was to be called the *Nakaz,* or *The Great Instruction.* It was nothing less than a complete revision and codification of Russian law. Catherine's aim was to replace the chaos of ancient legal tradition–often brutal and arbitrary–with a body of laws founded on Western European Enlightenment principles, especially as articulated by Montesquieu. His message to all sovereigns was that they must cultivate, disseminate, and defend a spirit of enlightened rationality throughout their realms. The sovereign's duty, he argued, was not to bring about sudden and destructive revolution, but to create the conditions under which society could be gradually remolded. This meant doing everything to create a climate of popular opinion that is receptive to enlightened ideas of social order and individual liberty.

Catherine was sincere in her desire to improve the lot of her subjects. She also saw *The Great Instruction* as an opportunity to elevate Russia within the family of nations. She intended the "immense work" to be circulated throughout the world as an example of what a Russian sovereign could create and what the Russian people, at all levels of society, were eager to embrace.

Catherine began composition of the *Nakaz* in 1764, and by 1766 she was passing around the manuscript to her advisers. Its final version, published in 1767, consisted of twenty-two chapters and 655 articles. As Catherine had hoped, it became an international bestseller. Widely translated, it circulated throughout Europe and even reached North America, on the verge of its own revolution.

> **Be ambitious.** Embrace works that promise to create influence and bring change. Examine each idea you have, every plan you formulate, and think of ways to make them more important, more enduring, more significant. Cultivate an "immense" vision. Create projects commensurate with its immensity.

■

Lesson 49

Create a Breakthrough

> "[The *Nakaz,* or *The Great Instruction* is] a masculine, nervous Performance, and worthy of a great man. . . . We have never heard of any Female being a Lawgiver. This Glory was reserved for the Empress of Russia."
>
> ~Frederick the Great, on Catherine's "immense" codification of Russian law, *The Great Instruction,* 1770

Catherine II intended, first and foremost, for her work on Russian law to transform the empire's ancient, even barbaric, legal chaos into a body of rational laws that could serve as models for any "enlightened" state in Western Europe. In this, she succeeded to a remarkable degree. Even more, however, *The Great Instruction* created for Russia a breakthrough image while simultaneously elevating Catherine to a status equal to that of a strong, wise, just, *male* ruler.

The shadow of Peter the Great, who had reigned from 1682 to 1725, was long. The likes of Empress Elizabeth and Peter III looked small and insignificant in its shade. With *The Great Instruction,* Catherine's model of government–more fully founded on enduring Enlightenment principles than Peter's "enlightened" despotism–dispelled the long shadow as she began to recreate Russia in her own image.

The most ambitious leaders of enterprise aim to leave their imprint on their organization. A minority succeed. An even smaller minority succeed in making their mark, not only in a way that improves the enterprise's outward image, but also in a way that improves the lives of people within that enterprise. This is the essence of a true breakthrough.

Catherine combined bold and generous vision with vigorous action and enduring expression—*The Great Instruction*—to impress her personality on her empire in a way that, not only rehabilitated Russia in the eyes of the world, but also made it a better place for those who lived in it.

■

Lesson 50
Be Grateful for Your Enemies

> "If we are successful in this war [against the Ottoman Empire], I shall have much to thank my enemies for: they will have brought me a glory to which I never aspired."
>
> ~Catherine, letter to Voltaire, October 1768

Far from expressing hatred of her country's traditional enemy, Ottoman Turkey, Catherine saw the opportunity to struggle against this foe as a valuable means of attaining victory in the eyes of the world.

> **It is through** confronting determined opposition that we become stronger, by learning to overcome and to prevail. Without enemies, few leaders achieve enduring recognition for their achievements. Resistance builds will, determination, strength, resourcefulness, and wit. Be grateful for the opposition you meet. Welcome it as an opportunity that you cannot create on your own.

■

Lesson 51
Perform a Reality Check

> "[Diderot's *Observations* is] a piece of genuine twaddle in which can be found neither knowledge of circumstances nor prudence nor perspicacity."
>
> ~Catherine, on Denis Diderot's criticisms of her treatise, *The Great Instruction,* about 1785

Since the beginning of her reign, Catherine had been corresponding with the greatest thinkers of the French

Enlightenment, including Voltaire, Rousseau, and Denis Diderot, who was coeditor of the monumental *Encyclopédie* and author of theoretical treatises on a great many subjects, ranging from art, to science, to politics.

Catherine admired Diderot's intellect, and she hosted him most cordially when he arrived in St. Petersburg on September 28, 1773. He was her guest for five months. Catherine relished long philosophical discussions with Diderot and later employed him to select the choicest European artworks for her collection (which became the basis of the celebrated Hermitage Museum, today one of the largest and oldest of the world's museums of art). When Diderot fell on hard times in Paris, Catherine purchased his library for a generous sum, yet did not collect the books while he still lived. Instead, she paid him to serve as the librarian of "her" library–in Paris. Nevertheless, Catherine was often uncomfortable with Diderot's probing questions about her governance, and particularly about her continued support for serfdom. For his part, despite his often critical questioning, Diderot admired Catherine, writing to friends that she possessed "the soul of Caesar with all the seductions of Cleopatra." Yet his assessment of her was ultimately ambivalent. He went on to declare that she possessed "the soul of Brutus in the body of Cleopatra." Thus, for him, she contained the soul of the great Roman Empire builder–as well as that of his assassin.

For her part, Catherine ultimately tempered admiration of Diderot's intellect with a brutally frank and unmistakably irritable assessment of his practical limitations. Diderot meticulously annotated *The Great Instruction* with critical remarks he must genuinely have believed she would find helpful. Instead, shortly after Diderot's death, Catherine privately dismissed them as "twaddle," deficient in "knowledge of circumstances," prudence, and perspicacity.

It is difficult to discern how much of Catherine's response was that of a sensitive author defending her two-year literary labor and how much was an objective assessment of the criticism. There is no doubt that Diderot made little effort to learn much about conditions in Russia, despite his five-month stay. So his "knowledge of circumstances" was, as Catherine wrote, indeed lacking. As for "prudence" and "perspicacity" (by which Catherine presumably meant astuteness and shrewdness), it is also quite likely that the philosopher in Diderot was incompatible with certain practical realities. It is clear that Catherine would have loved to apply theory directly to governance, but the more she tried, the more convinced she became that her aspiration to rule as a philosopher-monarch often collided with the hard, practical details of managing and administering a vast and often troubled empire.

Proverbs 29:18 puts it this way: "Where there is no vision, the people perish . . ." A vision of leadership embodying ideas, ideals, and theory is crucial to the health of any high-stakes collaborative endeavor. Yet when vision collides with certain rock-hard aspects of the real world, a thorough knowledge of circumstances and the possession of both discretion and discernment must trump philosophy—at least for the time being.

Check your most cherished theories against the real circumstances in which you must apply them. Do this repeatedly and often.

■

Lesson 52
Accelerate and Facilitate

> "We shall have [Princess Sophie of Württemburg] here within ten days. As soon as we have her, we shall proceed with her conversion. To convince her, it ought to take about fifteen days, I think. I do not know how long will be necessary to teach her to read intelligibly and correctly the confession of faith in Russian. But the faster this can be hurried through, the better. . . . To accelerate that [a cabinet secretary] has [already been sent] . . . to teach her the alphabet and the confession en route [to St. Petersburg]; conviction will follow afterwards. Eight days from this, I fix the wedding. If you wish to dance at it, you will have to hurry."
>
> ~Catherine, letter to Friedrich Melchior, baron von Grimm, August 1776, concerning the prospective bride to her son, Paul

Catherine's letter to Baron von Grimm, a prominent author and close associate of Rousseau, was written only partly tongue in cheek. Having come to the Russian throne by coup d'état, she was urgently concerned to establish an orderly and natural succession.

At the time, there was no question that her son would inherit the throne. Nevertheless, Catherine looked beyond him to *his* successors, and she was therefore anxious to get Paul suitably married. Her first choice had been Wilhelmina Louisa, daughter of Ludwig IX, the landgrave of Hesse-Darmstadt. She was given the Russian name Natalia Alexeievna, and Paul married her in 1773. Three years later, on April 15, 1776, both she and her son died in childbirth.

Paul was heartbroken, but Catherine, though saddened, was focused on perpetuating the royal line. She immediately made arrangements to connect Paul with Princess Sophie of Württemburg, whom Catherine had actually preferred over Wilhelmina Louisa in 1773, but who had been disqualified because she was just fourteen at the time. Now she was a marriageable seventeen, and Catherine quickly arranged a betrothal.

"She is precisely that which is desired," Catherine wrote to her Hamburg friend Frau Bielke, "shapely as a nymph, a complexion the color of the lily and the rose, the most beautiful skin in the world, tall, but still graceful." In her face were reflected "modesty, sweetness, kindness, and innocence." Indeed, Catherine believed, the "whole world is enchanted with her . . . she does everything to please."

"In a word," Catherine concluded to Frau Bielke, "my princess is everything that I desired."

Fortunately for Catherine's plans, *her* princess, who was everything *she* desired, also happened to be enormously attractive to Paul. With Sophie having accepted conversion from Lutheranism to the Russian Orthodox faith as Maria Fyodorovna, the couple was married just five months after Natalia's death.

For Catherine, nothing was more important than legitimating her ascension to power by ensuring the creation of an uncontested line of succession. As with Empress Elizabeth, it was so high a priority that she—repeating the history that brought about her own royal destiny—did everything possible to accelerate and facilitate a union of marriage likely to produce heirs. Catherine understood that, as an "absolute" ruler, there was much she could accomplish merely by commanding it. She also understood that, where emotion, nature, and destiny were concerned, the power of command was not sufficient. In these cases, she did all that *was* within her power to persuade, to enable, to facilitate, and to accelerate circumstances and events, arranging them as best she could to achieve the outcome she desired—and to do so with minimum delay.

Even the most powerful CEO has limited power and is rarely in a position to command precisely the outcomes he or she desires. The next best thing is to command what is within your power, creating an environment that makes the desired outcomes more probable than they would be if left to chance and the will of others.

■

Lesson 53

You Know What to Do

> "I suppose you know that the Turks have violated the peace with our empire and have even dared to incarcerate in the Castle of the Seven Towers a minister of MINE. You yourselves are to consider which measures ought to be taken from My side in such circumstances."
>
> ~Catherine, speech to her cabinet secretaries, 1788

In 1787, Catherine's triumphal tour of the Crimea–which she had recently annexed to the empire–in company with Joseph II of Austria, provoked the Sublime Porte (the Ottoman government) to break the treaty that had ended the Russo-Turkish War of 1768–1774 and once again declare war. The empress responded by delivering a short speech to her cabinet in the Winter Palace, in which she accused the Turks of having "violated the peace" and having imprisoned Ambassador Yakov Bulgakov ("a minister of MINE"). Instead of directing what action the cabinet should take, Catherine–having emphasized that, not only had the sovereignty of the empire been violated, but that a hostile act had been committed against *her*–deliberately left it up to her ministers to "consider which measures ought to be taken from My side."

The result was a new, aggressive war, and it was the result Catherine had expected. She understood that her ministers would act to defend, not just the Russian Empire, but their beloved monarch as well. She also understood the importance of ostensibly leaving this momentous decision to them, knowing that people are most enthusiastic about acting upon ideas they perceive as their own.

> **Usually, clear and** specific management direction is of the essence. In some situations, however, it is even more effective to fully outline a situation, make clear in your presentation both how the *organization* is affected and how *you* feel about it, but then leave the details of an effective solution to members of your team. The degree to which you can effectively outline your desired course of action, while making it feel like the team's idea and responsibility, should correlate to the commitment you can expect in the execution of the policy, program, project, or campaign. Full and free buy-in is always preferable to mere compliance, and the surest means to such buy-in is to create the conditions in which your team feels that it owns concepts, actions, events, and outcomes.

■

Lesson 54
Distinguish "Heat Lightning" from Thunder

> "I little . . . respect the French thunder or, better to say, heat lightning."
>
> ~Catherine, dispatch to her chief adviser Grigory Potemkin, April 14, 1783

As Catherine laid plans to go to war against the Ottoman Empire for a second time, with the purpose of securing territorial gains Russia had made in its earlier war against the Turks, her adviser Grigory Potemkin raised the specter of French sympathy for–even alliance with–the Ottoman Empire. To this, Catherine replied that she had "little . . . respect for the French thunder," then corrected herself by downgrading that thunder to mere "heat lightning."

Her metaphor was significant. Whereas thunder is more frightening than actually destructive, it does often herald a genuine storm. Heat lightning, on the other hand, is a property of distant thunderstorms that are too far away to be heard, and, thus, it announces no imminent threat. Catherine had analyzed the prospects of Catholic France actually aligning with Muslim Turkey against another Christian nation and concluded that, no matter how much noise the French emperor made at the present time, his country would not intervene militarily in a Russo-Turkish war.

Separate threatening noises from actual threats. Ignore the noise, so that you can put all your energy into planning effective responses to the genuine threats. In the first case, refuse to be paralyzed by apprehension. In the second, engage reality fully and make your decisions accordingly.

■

Lesson 55
Recruit Allies, but Don't Rely on Them

> "I rely little on an ally . . ."
>
> ~Catherine, dispatch to Grigory Potemkin, April 14, 1783

Much of Catherine's reign was focused on generally raising Russia's standing within the family of nations. She also worked hard to develop more specific strategic alliances. Catherine believed that isolation, which many of her predecessors had valued and acted to perpetuate, was fatal to the empire.

Despite her open orientation to the world, Catherine also announced to her top general, primary counselor, and virtual consort, Grigory Potemkin, her firm resolve "not to count on anybody but ourselves." In her second war with the Ottoman Empire, she made clear that she would press the campaign against the Turks with or without the collaboration of Austria. Her defiance was not reckless; it was founded on history. Based on prior victories, she fully believed that, even standing alone, Russia possessed the capability to defeat the Ottoman forces.

> **Forming strategic alliances** and partnerships is often critical to a business plan. Strategic thinking means, in part, thinking beyond the confines of your own organization. Fail to do this, and you risk losing many opportunities. Nevertheless, the core of your strategic thinking must never rely on allies. Partnerships based on dependency rather than independent strength are fraught with the highest risk for the least reward. Emulate Catherine by using allies to build the independence of your enterprise. Embark on joint ventures only when they help you to stand on your own.

■

Lesson 56

Bake the Cake

> "When the cake will be baked, each will have an appetite."
>
> ~Catherine, dispatch to Grigory Potemkin, April 14, 1783

In her plan to wage renewed war against the Ottoman Empire in 1783 (the actual war would span 1787–1792) to retain the lands she had won in the Russo-Turkish War of 1768–1774, Catherine II maneuvered diplomatically to secure an alliance with Austria.

Simultaneously, she prepared Russia to fight (and win) the war alone, if necessary. She explained to Potemkin that she was "firmly resolved not to count on anybody but ourselves," but, at the same time, she believed that, even if Russia commenced the war alone, early victories would ultimately attract alliances: "When the cake will be baked," she declared, "each will have an appetite."

Her strategy proved successful. The second war with the Ottoman Empire resulted not only in the confirmation of earlier Russian conquests but also the acquisition of the Yedisan region, encompassing southwestern Ukraine and southeastern Moldavia, thereby consolidating Russia's militarily and economically crucial connections with the West.

Preparation for any high-stakes action is important, but an obsessive focus on preparation should never be allowed to block the action itself. Demonstrated results are often critical to overcoming inertia in potential partners and allies. Wait for everyone at the table to get hungry, and you may go without eating. Sometimes you just have to bake the cake first. Just be certain you have all the necessary ingredients on hand—without having to beg them from neighbors.

■

Lesson 57

Pace Yourself

> "Everything do I see and hear, although I do not run, like the Emperor."
>
> ~Catherine, comment on the Austrian emperor Joseph II's early-morning hours, May 13, 1787

Having ordered and achieved the conquest and annexation of southern Ukraine from the Ottoman Empire, Catherine II toured the city of Kherson with her ally, the Habsburg emperor Joseph II of Austria. In contrast to the emperor, who peevishly complained about the city–deeming it crowded, noisy, and hot–but insisted on rising very early so that he could tour it beginning at six in the morning, Catherine took a more stately approach to enjoying a town she found quite to her liking. It was not that she was lazy–far from it, she saw and heard everything in the conquered city–but she did not believe that frenetic activity was necessary to demonstrate an astute interest in the events swirling about her. She preferred to pace herself, emanating a cool sense of control.

Vigorous management is not the same as running around wide-eyed. Stay alert, attend to situations promptly, look, listen, and understand. Pace yourself for a marathon, not a sprint. Joseph II did reign for a quarter century, but he was only forty-nine when he died. Catherine II, who ruled the Russian Empire for thirty-four years, lived to the age of sixty-seven—an enviable lifespan in eighteenth-century Russia.

■

Lesson 58
Intimidate Your Competitor

> "This man is extremely capable of multiplying fear and trembling in the foe . . ."
>
> ~Catherine to Grigory Potemkin, concerning the naval commander John Paul Jones, April 24, 1788

John Paul Jones, the Scottish-born hero of the American Revolution, found himself at loose ends in 1783, when his commission in the Continental Navy expired. The empress hired him to serve as a rear admiral in her imperial navy in 1788. His mission, Catherine dreamed, was to capture Constantinople, capital of the Ottoman Empire. "Paul Jones has arrived," she wrote on April 24, 1788. "I saw him today. I believe he will make a miracle here."

After fighting in the battle of Liman on the Black Sea and defeating Ottoman forces in the area, he soon fell victim to Potemkin's jealousy and was removed from command. While awaiting a new assignment, Jones was framed for the rape of a twelve-year-old girl in April 1789. To his credit, Potemkin personally investigated the allegations and, finding them baseless, ordered all charges dropped. By way of compensation, Catherine awarded Jones the Order of St. Anne on June 8, 1788. But it was too late. An aggrieved John Paul Jones left Russia the very next month.

Although the Russian naval career of America's greatest seafaring hero proved abortive, Catherine was correct about Jones's value as a weapon of intimidation. During the American Revolution, he had earned international renown as virtually a one-man navy, and Catherine was determined to make use of this reputation to "psych out" Ottoman naval leaders. She recognized Jones as what today's military leaders would call a "force multiplier"–that is, a person, situation, or other factor that dramatically increases the effectiveness of whatever military resources one has at hand.

Identify the force multipliers (assets whose impact is many times greater than their face value) available to you, and use them openly to intimidate your competitors. Anything that tends to undermine an opponent's morale degrades his capacity to attack you. New hires, new equipment, new products, and even a formidable record of past successes—all of these can be deployed as force multipliers against a competitor.

The Strategic Appeaser

CATHARINE II. ALEXIEVNA. EMPRESS OF RUSSIA. REIGNED XXXV YEARS.

Lesson 59
You Can Be Right, or You Can Be Successful

> "[Grand Duke Peter] always innocently believed that everyone was of his opinion and that there was nothing more natural. I took good care not to share his remarks with anyone, but I did not fail to reflect seriously on the destiny that awaited me."
>
> ~*Memoirs,* 1759–1794

Catherine recognized her husband, Grand Duke Peter, as precisely the opposite of herself. Whereas she worked hard to maintain a high level of discretion–carefully guarding her speech, taking care to offend no one at court–he "was naturally as discreet as a cannon blast, and when he had a heavy heart and something on his mind, he could not wait to recount it to those with whom he was accustomed to speak, *without considering to whom he spoke*" (emphasis added). Catherine understood that Peter, a pathologically self-absorbed man with little imagination and even less empathy, simply assumed that everyone believed as he did.

For her part, Catherine took care never to challenge Peter. Moreover, she protected him by resolutely refusing to "share his remarks with anyone." She "resolved to show great consideration for the grand duke's confidence," specifically "so that he would at least view me as someone he could trust, to whom he could say everything without any consequences."

It was, she wrote in her *Memoirs*, a deception in which she "succeeded . . . for a long time." There was, after all, nothing to be gained by asserting herself and embarrassing him by demonstrating that she was right and he was wrong. He, not she, was next in line for the throne. He, not she, was slated to inherit the power. Nevertheless, she did not let herself fall victim to her own deception. "I did not fail to reflect seriously on the destiny that awaited me," she wrote.

Catherine's attitude toward Grand Duke Peter–from this remove in history, a loser if there ever was one–was to make him feel as good about himself as possible. She had nothing to gain by proving herself right and him wrong. Her wagon, at least for the time being, was hitched to his star, and she would rise or fall by him. She also came to realize that he, and anyone associated with him, would ultimately fall, but until she was in a position to acquire her own power, she had to choose the path of most probable success rather than the path of a zero-sum victory that would most likely bring her down.

It is no secret that lawyers are generally unpopular. The reason is not that they're bad or dishonest people—they are neither less good nor less honest than those in any other profession. Lawyers do, however, put a high premium on winning—and winning for its own sake—which sometimes makes them look bad or dishonest.

In business, unlike in the courtroom, winning isn't everything—at least not if you see victory as a zero-sum game: For you to win, someone else must lose. In business, most often, success is measured not by *who* wins but by *how many* stakeholders gain. The most successful solutions are those that create the greatest value for the greatest number. In other words, successful businesses produce the most winners.

Make decisions and take actions that create as many winners as possible, yourself among them. This often entails putting your pride aside in times of dispute and seeking compromises that allow business operations to move forward. In any enterprise, where multiple differing opinions are invariably encountered, compromise and collaboration are vital to success. Leave the zero-sum game to the courtroom.

Lesson 60
Allow for Emotion

> "In spite of all the finest maxims of morality, whenever emotion has anything to do with the matter, one is already much further involved than one realizes."
>
> ~*Memoirs, 1759–1794*

Catherine understood emotion as a powerful force and therefore never made the mistake of discounting it when she made decisions and judged motives, whether those of others or her own. She scoffed at people who claimed that a strong sense of morality or rationality could neutralize the role of emotion in the choices people make, confessing, "I have still not learned how to prevent emotion being excited. Flight, perhaps, is the only remedy. But there are cases and circumstances, in which flight is impossible. For how can one escape, fly, or turn one's back, in the middle of a court?"

In fact, Catherine believed that "nothing is more difficult . . . than to escape from something that essentially attracts you. All statements made to the contrary will appear only a prudishness quite out of harmony with the natural instincts of the human heart." And the heart? It cannot, Catherine wrote, be held "in one's hand, tightening or relaxing one's grasp at will."

Armed with a frank and open understanding of the power of emotion, Catherine neither attempted to deny it (which would be futile) nor to escape it (which would be impossible). Instead, she figured it into every major decision she made and every piece of business she transacted. Her sense of what was best for the country, her support for the construction of hospitals and schools, as well as her drive to "Westernize" (in other words, modernize) Russian culture, were all driven by an essential compassion. The project of reform for which she became best known, the effort to rationalize Russia's medieval legal code, was no mere intellectual effort, but the product of an intense hatred of injustice and a feeling that cruelly archaic laws created a nation of unhappy, unbalanced people. It is also no accident that her very closest advisers, throughout her long reign, included her romantic intimates.

Business, like every other collective human enterprise, is driven by a range of motives, including a range of emotions, that are often beyond the reach of bottom-line calculations and any of the other "rational" factors that (we are told) should—to the exclusion of all other motives—enter into business. Catherine understood that states do not interact with other states. Rather, monarchs, ministers, and generals—that is, *people*—interact with other people. The relations between states, no matter how great and powerful, are therefore at least partially driven by the emotions of the people representing those states.

Carry the empress's understanding into your formulation of business: No company interacts with another company. All business is people business, and that means that all business has a component of emotion, passion, fear, anger, affection, attraction, and repulsion. You cannot run away from it, but you can attempt to calculate it in order to make decisions that win hearts and minds, building business person by person and person to person.

■

Lesson 61
Say the Right Thing

> "A mother gets angry and scolds her children and then it passes. . . . [Y]ou should have said to her . . . 'we beg your pardon, mother,' and you would have disarmed her."
>
> ~Advice recorded in *Memoirs,* 1759–1794

Madame Krause (or Kruse), appointed as Grand Duchess Catherine's lady-in-waiting, gave the young woman invaluable advice on how to assuage the anger of Empress Elizabeth. As a czar regarded himself as the "father" of the Russian people, so an empress saw herself as their "mother." Madame Krause advised Catherine to get in synch with this thinking, regard the empress as a mother, and speak to her as such. She provided a formulaic phrase to use whenever she happened to cross Elizabeth: "We beg your pardon, mother"–or, more accurately, "little mother" *(matushka),* a diminutive endearment. Catherine discovered that it worked like magic.

Know what people want to hear. Know why they want to hear it. Whenever you can, say precisely what they want to hear. This is not a license to lie or to withhold important information, but it is useful to apply this formula in as many situations as possible. Doing so may require a strenuous exercise of creative imagination that identifies a path from failure to success. If, for example, an employee performs an assignment unsatisfactorily, it will not do the employee or your organization any good to assure him that he has performed admirably. At the same time, mere condemnation, while truthful, will only dishearten. What the employee *wants* to hear is that he *can* succeed. Look for a way to criticize *and* motivate simultaneously: "You and I both agree that the project has produced disappointing results. I am confident that you will deliver better results next time if you review the customer feedback. Give me a report, and let's work out a new plan before you relaunch."

■

Lesson 62
Exploit Weakness

> "Everyone feared [Madame Choglokova and her husband as vengeful spies for Empress Elizabeth]. However, there were ways . . . not only to put these Arguses to sleep but even to win them over. . . . One of the surest was to play faro with them; they were both gamblers and very intense ones at that. This weakness was the first discovery; others came later."
>
> ~ *Memoirs,* 1759–1794

In the years before she ascended the throne, Catherine found herself under continual scrutiny by agents of Empress Elizabeth. Hardly neutral figures, they all tended to be treacherous and vindictive. Catherine judged the Choglokovas to be "truly wicked," and she was not the only member of the imperial court who feared them. Instead of simply avoiding the couple, however, Catherine carefully observed them and soon concluded that they both suffered from a weakness for faro, a popular card game that they played compulsively and for high stakes. A voracious reader, the last thing Catherine wanted to do with her free time was to play cards, especially with people she loathed. Nevertheless, she frequently engaged the Choglokovas in their game–a tactic that not only lulled them into inattention but made them more sympathetic to her.

Even the most formidable opponent has vulnerabilities and deficiencies that can be productively exploited. Discover them and use them to your advantage.

■

Lesson 63
Ask Questions

> "His Imperial Highness [Grand Duke Peter] came into my room and told me that I was becoming intolerably haughty and that he knew how to bring me back to my senses. I asked him what he meant by haughty. . . ."
>
> ~ *Memoirs,* 1759–1794

Catherine well knew that her husband was a cruel and unbalanced man. Told by others in Elizabeth's court that he was losing control of his wife, Peter physically threatened Catherine. The exchange began by his telling her she had become "intolerably haughty" and that "he knew how to bring [her] back to [her] senses."

Instead of apologizing, pleading for mercy, or responding with protests or argument, Catherine stood her ground simply by asking a question. What did he mean by "haughty"?

The answer he returned was absurd. He complained that Catherine held herself "very erect." Catherine did not respond with the laughter or scorn the accusation warranted, but with another question, asking if "one had to keep one's back bent like some great master's slave" in order to please him. To this, Peter responded by warning that "he well knew how to bring [her] back to [her] senses."

Continuing to stand firm, Catherine calmly asked him how. "At this," she wrote in her *Memoirs*, "he put his back against the wall and drew his sword halfway out and showed it to me." Even now, in the face of this dire physical threat, Catherine asked yet another question: Did he mean to fight her? "In that case, I would need [a sword] too," she reasoned.

In response, Peter returned his sword to its scabbard and then spat out that Catherine had "become dreadfully nasty."

Although he had shifted from threat to insult, Catherine maintained her own steady questioning course, asking him, "In what way?"

Peter "stammered" a vague complaint about her attitude toward a court couple, the Shuvalovs. With that, the heated exchange, deprived of its emotional fuel by Catherine's calm questions, simply trailed off. The storm had passed.

> **Questions are powerful** instruments as well as formidable weapons. In a dispute, they can produce answers, which means that they may lead to a productive resolution. Failing this, however, questions nevertheless compel your opponent to shift from emotion-driven behavior to some degree of thought. Ask the right questions, and you and your rival may reach a creative, collaborative understanding. Even if you do not, you may well succeed in countering or undermining his or her position by demonstrating that the grievance is flawed or even baseless. Challenged, resist the urge to cower in fear or to respond in anger. Instead, calmly but relentlessly question the motives and basis of your opponent's words and actions.

■

Lesson 64
Apply Facts

> "I told him that it was not I but the almanac that discredited what he was recounting . . ."
>
> ~*Memoirs,* 1759–1794

Among Grand Duke Peter's many flaws was his penchant for telling lies. Though frustrated by this habit, Catherine never accused her husband of lying. Instead, she applied common sense, reason, and facts to each of his dubious statements, so that they stood or fell by those objective measures.

In her *Memoirs,* she recounted an occasion on which her husband "dreamed up" a lie to "make himself appealing to some young woman or girl." Peter told her that while he was still living in Holstein, his father had put him in command of a squad of his guards and sent him to lead the capture of a troop of what Peter referred to as "Egyptians" (they may have been gypsies) who had committed robberies near Kiel. Peter narrated the details of his exploits, relying on the ignorance of the girl to prevent his being exposed as a liar.

Apparently, over time, he repeated the same story to others. At first, he made certain to tell it only "to people who knew nothing of the matter." Eventually, however, "he grew bold enough to recount his tale before those whose discretion he could trust would keep them from refuting him."

At last he made the mistake of telling it in Catherine's presence. She responded by asking how long before his father's death the events had taken place. Without hesitation, he answered three or four years. At this, she responded, "Well then, you began to accomplish your feats of arms very young, because three or four years before the death of your father . . . you were only six or seven."

Peter "got terribly angry" with Catherine, accusing her of wanting "to make him look like a liar in front of everyone." She responded that it was not she, but the almanac–a source of objective fact–that discredited him and that she "would let him judge for himself if it was humanly possible to send a little child of six or seven, an only son and hereditary Prince, his father's entire hope, to capture Egyptians." At this, the grand duke fell silent.

Never dispute a person. Instead, challenge facts with facts, common sense, and reason. Base no argument on subjective judgment, personality, or character. Argue from a position of objective measure and evaluation. In business, the strongest arguments are made in the language of business: money earned, money lost, money at risk, money saved, and the value received for money invested.

■

Lesson 65
Revalue Value to Your Advantage

> "I replied . . . that I was accustomed to regarding everything that came to me from Her Imperial Majesty's hands as priceless."
> ~*Memoirs,* 1759–1794

On one occasion, Empress Elizabeth presented young Catherine with the gift of a jewelry box that contained "a very poor little necklace with earrings and two pitiful rings that I would have been ashamed to give my ladies-in-waiting." Catherine judged that the box held "not a single stone worth a hundred rubles."

Keenly aware of the parsimonious nature of the imperial gift, a confidant of Elizabeth, Count Alexander Shuvalov, told Catherine that the empress had ordered him to "find out how I liked the box."

Asked this question under such circumstances, almost no one would tell the obvious truth: that the gift was at best disappointing and, at worst, an insult. A person of ordinary intelligence and judgment would simply lie, expressing feigned gratitude and praising the poor offerings extravagantly. Catherine, however, possessed more than ordinary intelligence and judgment. She knew that the empress would be insulted and angered by a lie—especially an obvious lie. She therefore delivered an answer that shifted the focus of the question from the gift to a definition of her own relationship with Empress Elizabeth. Instead of talking about the miserable jewels, she praised the value of any token bestowed by "Her Imperial Majesty's hands." Whatever the empress touched, whatever the empress gave, Catherine said, in effect, was made valuable beyond any intrinsic worth.

It was precisely the right answer, and it raised Catherine greatly in the esteem of Empress Elizabeth.

> **Success in business** often comes down to maximizing the perception of value. Make it a practice to increase the perception of the value of whatever assets you acquire, however you acquire them. Find ways to leverage even modest value to achieve important ends. Never be satisfied to accept the "set" or "intrinsic" value of an asset.

■

Lesson 66

Average the Extremes

> "In the one [Senate party] you will find persons of honest manners although shortsighted minds; in the other I think the views extend further, but it is unclear whether they are always practicable . . ."
>
> ~Catherine's instruction to Prince Aleksandr Vyazemsky, whom she appointed procurator-general of the Senate, September 1764

Shortly after taking power in Russia, Catherine removed the reputedly corrupt procurator-general (supervisor) of the Senate, Alexander Glebov, and replaced him with a newcomer to court politics, Prince Aleksandr Vyazemsky. She shared with the prince her opinion of the two prevailing parties, or factions, in the Senate. Catherine believed that the more conservative faction was honest but shortsighted and lacking in vision, whereas the more progressive faction was more visionary but often less practical. Instead of advising Vyazemsky as to which of the two was her favored party, Catherine admonished him to treat both equally, implying that she wanted to synthesize the most useful solutions from the two extremes. This was not merely a formula for compromise, but a genuine synthesis–useful in that the strengths of one party would tend to correct or compensate for the deficiencies of the other.

Our experience of American politics has taught us to take sides. Catherine harbored no such prejudice. She dealt with the opposing political factions in the Russian Senate by averaging out their differences in an effort to synthesize the most effective solutions to given issues.

Consider perhaps the single most polarizing social issue in Catherine's Russia: the status of serfs and serfdom. The most liberal elements in government advocated the abolition of serfdom, the most conservative sought to strengthen the institution of serfdom by further limiting the few rights serfs had (such as the right to accumulate wealth, even while bound to the land). Catherine formulated a middle course between the extremes, giving serfs the right to sue members of the landowning nobility in court if the landowner failed to honor agreements made with those who worked his land. This had the effect of giving the serfs standing within the system of the government, so that they were no longer entirely at the mercy of a landowner. The newly granted right made both serf and nobleman subjects of law—a law that otherwise reaffirmed the institution of serfdom.

Synthesis is a mode of dispute resolution as well as problem solving that any modern leader should carefully consider. Rather than simply dilute a position through compromise, this wise, impartial leader finds the strongest approach by borrowing the best from two or more differing proposals. Binary problem solving works efficiently for computers, but is usually less effective when human managers formulate approaches to human processes.

■

Lesson 67

Solve the Value Equation

> "Our just and merciful intention is to correct the simple and the errant, to defend the insulted, and to deflect direct attacks and oppressions on those peasants by means of the good arrangement of their work with beneficial pay, in proportion to their labors . . ."
>
> ~Catherine, manifesto addressed to rebellious peasants assigned to factory labor in the Urals, 1762

When peasant factory laborers (some were indentured laborers; others, outright serfs) rebelled in the Urals, they posed a grave threat to the Russian metals industry, the source of the empire's arms and coinage. The temptation was therefore strong to put down the rebellion by force. Instead, however, Catherine sent Prince Aleksandr Vyazemsky, a man she trusted as an observer and as a troubleshooter, to report to her on the crisis in detail. She sent him armed with a manifesto that called for the laborers to resume work and also pledged that their grievances would be addressed once they did go back to their jobs. The proposition Catherine offered them was an exchange of value for value. The workers would be protected from abuse by their employer-masters, and they would be paid fairly "in proportion to their labors."

This short-term solution, which substituted fairness for force, ended the strike. Catherine, however, also looked beyond the particular crisis to find a permanent solution to the national value equation. She ordered Vyazemsky to investigate the use of so-called bondaged peasant labor–an indentured or contractual form of labor that was a conditional serfdom–and to report on how the vital metallurgical industry could make the transition to using free labor exclusively.

Catherine understood this much about government as business: All relationships had to be based on mutually beneficial exchanges of value for value. Fail in this, and a government invited rebellion. Fail in this, and a business invites loss of workers, loss of investors, and loss of customers. A business that fails to exchange value for value is not a business, but a den of thieves.

■

Lesson 68

Be a King Maker

> "I am sending Count Keyserling immediately as ambassador to Poland to make you king after the death of Augustus III."
>
> ~Catherine, to Stanisłaus Poniatowski, December 1762

In 1762, King Augustus III of Poland was ailing and not expected to recover. Everyone, including the Polish people, believed that his son would succeed him. Catherine, however, was opposed to this because Frederick Christian was no great friend of Russia. She perceived that Adam Czartoryski, Poland's prince-chancellor, was a devoted Russophile, but he was also a strong figure with a fierce streak of independence and national pride. What Catherine wanted was a Russophile king who was also pliable. Her ideal candidate was Stanisłaus Poniatowski, a young Pole who had come to the court at St. Petersburg as an assistant to the British ambassador to Russia. He and Catherine became friends and then lovers, and even after Poniatowski had been forced to leave Russia, he remained devoted to her.

That he had no desire to be king of Poland hardly mattered to Catherine. He was a native Pole (which would please the Polish people) and conformable to her will (which pleased her). She therefore set about engineering his ascension to the Polish throne, whether he wanted it or not.

Catherine's first step was to appoint Hermann Karl von Keyserling as Russia's ambassador to Poland and to give him a 100,000-ruble budget for the purpose of bribing whomever he deemed necessary to ensure that Poniatowski was properly positioned to be chosen. But she did not rely on bribery alone. To move negotiations in her favor, she also immediately ordered thirty thousand Russian soldiers to her country's border with Poland.

With both funding and flintlocks in place, Catherine next prevailed on Frederick the Great of Prussia to support her choice. He was none too eager at first, but Catherine knew that Frederick was far more likely to endorse Poniatowski than would either Joseph II of Austria or Louis XVI of France. She therefore pressed her suit with him, pointing out that her choice would be good not only for Russia but also for Prussia as well. Frederick held out for a formal Russian-Prussian alliance before he would agree. Catherine responded with delaying tactics, and when Frederick finally showed signs of yielding to her, she pushed him past the tipping point by finally agreeing to an alliance. In response, the Prussian king threw his wholehearted support behind Poniatowski. The Poles, now under military threat from these allies, negotiated a treaty with Russia and Prussia, secretly agreeing to the succession of Catherine's candidate. Negotiations were still underway, however, when Augustus III died in October 1763, and Catherine was obliged to invest more bribery money to ensure the treaty's finalization. The Polish parliament–the Sejm–elected Stanisłaus Poniatowski king on September 7, 1764.

Give your support and exercise your influence to elevate your allies to positions of power. Play an active role in creating leadership environments most favorable to you and your enterprise.

■

Lesson 69

Recruit and Reward Service

> "By this institution, We give to Our people an example of our sincerity, of our great belief in them, and of our true Maternal love."
>
> ~Catherine, manifesto introducing the creation of representatives ("deputies") to assist in the formulation of specific laws in accordance with *The Great Instruction,* December 14, 1766

Catherine's monumental revision of Russian law–her *Great Instruction,* or *Nakaz*–laid down the basis for specific laws, the creation of which she saw as a collaboration among herself, her advisers, the Senate, and, in a groundbreaking action for Russia, a set of representatives, or deputies, selected from all the legally recognized classes of Russia, including the peasants but not the serfs. One of the most formidable obstacles this innovation in Russian government had to overcome was a traditional feeling among the people to regard civil service and service in appointed or elective offices as burdensome. In response, Catherine created a system of recognition and reward for those who served. Deputies were decorated with a special badge, and they received lifelong immunity from judicial torture, corporal punishment, and capital punishment. They were also well paid for their services. Nobles received 400 rubles annually, townspeople received 122, and peasants, 37 rubles. Armed with these incentives, Catherine also expressed her belief in her people. Thus, the employment of deputies not only added valuable representative input into the creation of the empire's laws, it also became an opportunity for Catherine to forge direct bonds with all classes of Russia. It was her opportunity to give more Russians a stake in *her* government and *her* authority.

Take every available opportunity to secure input from across your organization. Give as many people as practically possible a direct stake in *your* leadership. Sweeten all voluntary positions with tangible, valuable rewards. Engage your whole enterprise wherever and whenever you can.

■

Lesson 70

Get Input—without Relinquishing Control

> "[The Legislative Commission] appears to me in the light of a scaffolding to be removed of course when the Empress has completed the noble edifice She has planned, a code of laws upon her own principles, but in the manner most consistent with the true interest and the inclination of all her subjects."
>
> ~British ambassador, on the work of the Legislative Commission, December 1767, quoted in John T. Alexander, *Catherine the Great: Life and Legend*

After publishing her *Great Instruction,* the monumental revision of Russian law, Catherine took another momentous step in creating a "Legislative Commission" made up of representatives from all classes of the Russian people–nobles, townsmen, and peasants alike–to provide detailed input on creating specific laws. As the British ambassador to the Russian imperial court observed, however, this manifestation of representative government was a kind of "scaffolding" to be removed once the appropriate set of laws, created according to Catherine's principles, were in place.

Catherine wanted to hear from her subjects. As the ambassador observed, she was earnest in her intention of serving "the true interest and inclination of all her subjects," Nevertheless, she wanted to do so without conceding ultimate control of the government to any representative institution. If she was establishing a precedent of representative government, she took care to establish it as a precedent for *temporary* representation rather than as a permanent feature of her reign.

Some managers resist seeking input from the members of their team out of fear that doing so will force them to relinquish some degree of their autonomous authority. In fact, it is perfectly possible—and quite advantageous—to solicit input and feedback from "the troops" without transforming your management authority into leadership by consensus. The best decisions are made on the basis of the best information. The more input you obtain from all stakeholders, the more complete basis you establish from which to make the best leadership decisions possible. But, in order to avoid interminable delays resulting from the conflicts of interest between stakeholders, *you* must remain the one who makes those decisions.

■

Lesson 71

If You Must Take, Also Give

> "One might still also make harmless bonfires that serve the spectators' satisfaction and cleanse the air . . ."
>
> ~Catherine, measures proposed to curb epidemic disease in Moscow, Letter to Sergei Saltykov, April 12, 1771

Although eighteenth-century medicine had not arrived at the germ theory of infection, it was generally accepted that indoor crowding promoted the spread of epidemic disease. Accordingly, Catherine recommended measures to reduce public assembly indoors. This included banning masquerades and theatrical entertainments. Even as she suggested this ban, however, she recognized that it might well provoke popular protest and undermine public morale. She therefore recommended balancing the ban on indoor entertainment with outdoor amusements and opportunities for assembly.

"Public promenades especially are very good and can be expected to be filled with people, if various diversions are set up there," she wrote. She proposed "harmless bonfires," which would not only amuse ("serve the spectators' satisfaction") but would actually "cleanse the air" of what, at the time, were believed to be airborne "miasmatic" agents that transmitted disease.

While Catherine was eager to avoid angering or demoralizing the populace, she explained that her "main desire [was] to seek out modes for diminishing the action of the infection," and she pointed out that the means she prescribed "have often produced good successes in such circumstances in other lands."

For generations, people believed that the only effective medicines were bitter potions that tasted terrible. However, the general proposition that creating good requires pain is irrational and often flies in the face of reality. Also, the people on whom the "cure" is inflicted often do not accept this line of argument and, hence, will resist the unpleasant remedy.

Managers often need to take steps that are bound to receive little welcome. In these cases, it is necessary to explain the measures, with particular emphasis on why they are necessary and the benefits they will bring. If possible, sweeten any bitter medicine with a morale lifter. If, for example, a crunch deadline requires overtime, have a wonderful buffet meal sent up to the office. Even if you cannot provide something immediately tangible, when you present a measure likely to be unpopular, paint the benefits as vividly as possible and with the emphasis on just how those benefits will be of value to those most affected by the measure in question.

■

Lesson 72
Be Grateful

> "For all the labors exerted by you and the boundless cares for my affairs I cannot sufficiently expound my recognition to you; you yourself know how sensitive I am to merits, and yours are outstanding, just as my friendship and love for you are . . ."
>
> ~Catherine, letter to Grigory Potemkin, July 28, 1783

In 1783, during the interval between her two wars with the Ottoman Empire, Catherine's chief adviser, top military commander, and unofficial consort, Grigory Potemkin, often proved uncommunicative about the progress he was making in securing the submission and loyalty of the empire's recent

Crimean conquests. Anxious and provoked, Catherine suddenly turned a cold shoulder toward a man who was not only her confidante and lover, but the most efficient agent of her imperial ambitions. Wishing to repair the relationship, Catherine wrote a letter of appreciation and thanks to him.

More than anything, the empress's remarks demonstrated the depth of her awareness of just what Potemkin had achieved for her. She acknowledged Potemkin's "labors" and his "boundless cares," and she confessed that she could never "sufficiently expound" her "recognition" of them. She also reminded Potemkin of her sensitivity to merits–a way of assuring him that her praise and gratitude were not empty gestures, but rather genuine admiration that arose from the very core of her judgment about those who served her and the empire. She also took pains to express her assessment of his "outstanding" merits as directly proportionate to her "friendship and love" for him.

Grigory Potemkin could not doubt the depth and sincerity of Catherine's regard for him and for his performance. Armed with this knowledge, he could not but continue to serve with the greatest of confidence. To ensure that Potemkin would continue to act with aggressive vigor, Catherine concluded with a homely expression of her own confident expectations: "I know that you will not stick your face in the mud . . ."

Take time to acknowledge the achievements of those on whom you rely. Be grateful, and also express that gratitude in ways that demonstrate its sincerity, depth, and basis in actual achievement. This is not mere flattery. It is a means of measuring performance that also provides incentive for even greater performance in the future. By expressing your confidence in a top performer, you demand top performance going forward.

Lesson 73
Unambiguously Delegate Authority

> "Be assured that I shall not subordinate you to anyone, except myself."
>
> ~Catherine, letter to Grigory Potemkin, July 28, 1783

In a 1783 letter to Grigory Potemkin, who at the time was putting out political fires in the Crimea, Catherine delivered a remarkable vote of confidence. She assured him that she would not subordinate him to anyone–except herself.

Her delegation of authority was precise and conferred without the least ambiguity (obscurity of meaning) or ambivalence (mixed emotions). She announced to him that he was to serve no one but herself. There were no *ifs, ands,* or *buts.*

With authority come exposure and the potential for blame. Authority is therefore desired and avoided. Because it is subject to ambiguity in interpretation and to ambivalence in execution, authority comes sown with numerous booby traps. These can be reduced, perhaps even removed entirely, if you take care to delegate authority with absolute clarity.

■

The Enlightened Empress

CATHARINE II. ALEXIEVNA. EMPRESS OF RUSSIA. REIGNED XXXV YEARS.

Lesson 74
Open Ears, Open Mind

> "Monsieur Pechlin made clear to the Grand Duke that to listen was not to negotiate, that negotiation was far from agreement, and that he would always have the power to break off the discussions when he judged it appropriate."
>
> ~Monsieur Pechlin, minister for Grand Duke Peter's duchy of Holstein, quoted in Catherine's *Memoirs,* 1759–1794

Pechlin had a great deal of difficulty persuading Grand Duke Peter to listen to a proposal from Denmark to avoid war over Danish possession of the grand duke's Holstein-Gottorp lands. In fact, with his mind set on waging a war (for which he was totally unprepared), the grand duke initially refused even to hear the Danish proposal. At this point, Pechlin delivered a lesson on the low cost of listening and keeping an open mind.

It was a lesson Catherine also heard, and she would never forget it. The decision to listen is a decision to acquire information and thereby enlarge one's knowledge and perspective. It need never imply agreement with a rival, let alone surrender.

No good decision can be made in ignorance of key facts and conditions. Whatever your present convictions, listening costs you nothing. Opening your mind is free of obligation. You may not be able to avoid prejudging a situation, but you can withhold acting upon your prejudgment. Listen. If appropriate, proceed to negotiation. Neither step entails ultimate agreement, but both steps are necessary to gather the facts and conditions on which informed and effective plans are built.

Lesson 75
Do Justice

> "You see, they say that they suspect him of embezzlement."
> ~Grand Duke Peter, quoted in *Memoirs,* 1759–1794

One day, Grand Duke Peter informed Catherine that "he was being told" that "it was absolutely necessary for him to send a secret order to Holstein [his duchy] to arrest a man named d'Elendsheim."

Recognizing the name as that of a most prominent figure, Catherine asked what the "grievances" were against him. The grand duke replied, "They say that they suspect him of embezzlement."

"They" was insufficient for Catherine, who asked just who the accusers were. To her astonishment, Peter replied that there were "no accusers, because everyone in the country fears and obeys [d'Elendsheim], and for this reason," it was necessary to arrest the man. After a pause, the grand duke added that *after* the arrest he was "assured that there will be more than enough accusers."

Catherine recorded in her *Memoirs* that she "shuddered" at what her husband said. To him, she replied, "But if one acts in this manner, there will be no more innocent people in the world. All it takes is one jealous person to spread publicly whatever vague rumor pleases him, at which they will arrest whomever they want, saying that the accusers and the crimes will appear later." She told her husband that he was being "advised to act without regard either for your glory or your justice."

As empress of Russia, Catherine would enjoy absolute power, by tradition and by law. She never took this as license to abandon the principles of truth, evidence, and justice, however. In part, she was motivated by a strong sense of ethics, but she also understood that her authority rested on law and that if she herself abrogated law, she would destroy the very foundation of her own rule.

Accept the limits of power on which your authority is based. To do justice is to reinforce your authority. To exercise your authority without regard for justice will damage your "glory" and, hence, destroy your authority.

■

Lesson 76

Be Relentlessly Curious

"You always want to know more than the others."

~Grand Duke Peter, complaining to Catherine, quoted in *Memoirs,* 1759–1794

Grand Duke Peter was not interested in devoting much thought to his actions. Nor did he like to be questioned about what he did or proposed to do. Told that one d'Elendsheim, an official in his duchy of Holstein, *needed* to be arrested on suspicion of embezzlement, he did not bother to ask who the accusers were or to demand evidence. He heard the demands for the man's arrest and was ready to have him arrested. When Catherine objected, asking the grand duke to reveal who had demanded the arrest, Peter replied peevishly, "You always want to know more than the others."

"You always want to know more than the others." As if that were a bad thing! Curiosity is an essential component in the personality of any effective leader. On what basis can sound management and visionary leadership be founded *other than* the desire to "know more than the others"? Curiosity and an insatiable appetite for facts are essential to the successful leadership of any enterprise. Decision without knowledge leads, in the absence of extraordinary good luck, to catastrophe.

■

Lesson 77
Limit Your Power

> "The Empress professed notions sometimes termed 'democratic autocracy,' in her desire 'to be worthy of the love of Our people' . . ."
>
> ~Comment on Catherine's manifesto, published on assuming the throne, July 9, 1762, in John T. Alexander, *Catherine the Great: Life and Legend*

Historians have described most of the reign of Catherine the Great using the oxymoronic phrase "democratic autocracy." She herself took the title of "autocratrix," as if to imply the complete independence of her authority. Yet she declared that her intention was always "to be worthy of the love of Our people." Without question, she intended to rule as an absolute sovereign, but she resolved to do so within the limits established by the nation's religion, culture, and traditions, as these were informed by Enlightenment ideas of government expressed by Rousseau, Voltaire, Diderot, Montesquieu, and Locke–the very philosophers who would heavily influence the American Revolution and, later, the French Revolution.

Catherine was an ethical leader who genuinely had the welfare of her people at heart. She also saw self-imposed, transparent limits on her power as a means of ensuring her popular acceptance and endurance as empress. Having survived and ultimately risen in an imperial court into which she had arrived as an outsider, often shunned and excluded, Catherine had a deep appreciation for what it meant to have a stake in a great enterprise. Therefore, she was determined to make her absolute reign as open and as inclusive as possible–without undermining the finality of her autocratic authority.

> **Winners who take** all soon have nothing. Deprive the members of your organization of any stake in the well-being and prosperity of that organization, and you cannot expect to create voluntary compliance, let alone enthusiastic loyalty. Instead of *winner take all,* consider *winner gives much*. Limit your power, and you might sustain it for decades, as Catherine did.

■

Lesson 78
Use Celebration and Reward to Inspire Loyalty

> "Ballrooms were set up . . . . A fair was organized . . . there were fireworks . . . feasts, fountains flowing with wine . . . and buildings, serving as kitchens and for other purposes, were put up so that between sixty and one hundred thousand people could have all their wants supplied for between ten to twelve hours . . ."
>
> ~Catherine, letter to Voltaire describing the celebration of victory in the Crimea, July 1775

From July 10 through July 23, 1775, Catherine the Great authorized massive celebrations of Russia's victories in the Crimea, which acquired for the empire (among much else) a coveted port on the Black Sea. The celebrations showcased the presentation of lavish awards to all the field marshals, generals, admirals, and other architects of victory. For example, General Pyotr Rumyantsev, who led numerous successful military campaigns during the war, was presented with a diamond-encrusted commander's baton and sword, a crown of laurel leaves and an olive branch, the cross and star of the Order of the Apostle St. Andrew, five thousand serfs, 100,000 rubles to build a house, a silver service for the house's dining table, and a set of paintings to decorate the house.

Among the many contrasts between the leadership styles of Catherine the Great and her mother-in-law, the notoriously parsimonious Empress Elizabeth, was Catherine's reliance on extravagant rewards for those who proved their loyalty to her, those who carried out her commands, and those who served her empire. She was lavish in her generosity. Moreover, the presentation of rewards was typically a very public event, often in the context of a massive celebration. In this way, Catherine leveraged the act of reward beyond the immediate recipient, transforming each occasion into a lesson for the nation: Serve your sovereign, serve your nation, and you will be more than amply repaid.

In the sharpest possible contrast, Empress Elizabeth relied almost exclusively on threats of punishment–midnight arrest, judicial torture, and imprisonment without hearing or trial–methods the czars had been using since the Middle Ages. Under Elizabeth, the Russian Empire retreated from the progress it had begun to achieve within the family of nations during the reign of Peter I (1682–1725), whereas, under Catherine II, the empire advanced even beyond what Peter had built. For this reason, Catherine shares with Peter the title of "the Great." Elizabeth? Her reign is barely remembered today by those without a special interest in Russian history.

As a leader, you can choose to compel obedience by means of threat, warning, and punishment, such as demotion or unfavorable assignments, or you can elicit cheerful and enthusiastic buy-in to your vision, objectives, and goals by celebrating and rewarding achievements. The latter approach surely will win you allies and support, helping to sustain your leadership and secure your legacy.

■

Lesson 79
Share Your Triumphs

> "To provide a treat for the people, a fairly large open space was chosen . . ."
>
> ~Catherine, letter to Voltaire describing the celebration of victory in the Crimea, July 1775

Prior to the ascension of Catherine II to the Russian imperial throne, governance in the nation was closed and secretive. None but the nobility was made to feel they had a stake in the fate of the country. Rule was autocratic in the strictest sense of the word, and authority, accordingly, was arbitrary.

In this government, power was held, not given.

No monarch holds power that is truly "absolute." In fact, authority is retained only as long as the sovereign possesses sufficient resources to coerce and compel obedience. Wielding authority over those who perceive no benefit for themselves in the monarch's policies is a strenuous and draining task, requiring a tremendous expenditure of energy. The fewer the stakeholders, the more intimidation and use of force is required to maintain authority.

It would be a very naïve error to assert that Catherine II transformed Russian history by bringing anything like modern democracy to the governance of the nation. She did no such thing. Nevertheless, she did transform Russia profoundly by opening up the government to a degree unprecedented at the time. She encouraged even the lowliest of her subjects to claim a stake in the fate of the empire and to perceive it as beneficial to them. When she staged a grand celebration in Moscow after the military and naval victories that resulted in the annexation of the Crimea and the acquisition of an all-important Black Sea port, she did so not merely for the entertainment and gratification of the noble and highborn. As she explained to her frequent correspondent Voltaire, she intended to "provide a treat for the people." Further, Catherine decided to dramatize the distant events to them, choosing (as she explained to Voltaire) "a fairly large open space . . . which we called 'the Black Sea' and covered with ships." The approach to this space, representative of the scene of victory, "was by two roads . . . Both . . . adorned with various scenes–farms, villages, windmills, etc." Everything was given a name borrowed from the conquered region, so that common people living in Moscow–people who would never venture to the Crimea–might themselves feel like conquerors. The celebratory space was arranged to accommodate at least one hundred thousand people, all of whom would "have all their wants supplied for between ten to twelve hours."

Celebrate the triumphs of your enterprise. This means *sharing* them with every stakeholder in your organization. If you would have them buy into your vision and goals, share successes in the most tangible ways possible, frequently.

■

Lesson 80

Don't Outsource Your Mind

> "For the past two months I have been busy working three hours every morning on the laws of this empire. It is an immense undertaking."
>
> ~Catherine, letter to Marie Thérèse Rodet Geoffrin, January 1765

In her *Memoirs,* Catherine was critical of Empress Elizabeth's practice of farming out the writing of state papers and official correspondence to others. Worse, when a ghostwritten paper was ready, she rarely even bothered to read it before signing, and even more rarely followed up on the implementation of its content. In contrast to both Elizabeth and Peter III, Catherine insisted on personally writing most of her own state papers and all of her correspondence. When she did delegate a writing assignment, she always reviewed and revised it carefully. Moreover, she was a stickler for details on which she followed through meticulously.

In fact, Catherine was an excellent writer, whose incomplete *Memoirs* is widely read and is still considered a significant contribution to eighteenth-century European literature. Her magnum opus, however, was her *Nakaz,* or *The Great Instruction,* a monumental compilation, rationalization, and revision of the laws of the Russian Empire–all of it based on her remarkable understanding of Enlightenment principles, embodied especially in the work of Charles-Louis de Secondat, baron de Montesquieu (mainly *The Spirit of Laws*) and the more pragmatic writing of the jurist and legal scholar Cesare Beccaria (*Essay on Crimes and Punishment*). The final version of *The Great Instruction,* which she composed over the course of two years, consisted of 655 articles in twenty-two chapters and was admired by figures as prominent and varied as Frederick the Great of Prussia and the French philosopher Voltaire.

Do as much of your own original and creative work as possible. Create your vision and then deliver it, fresh, in your own words. Colleagues, bosses, and customers recognize original thought and appreciate as well as admire it, even if they do not fully agree with it. What you write and publish becomes your brand. Shape, control, and protect it. Do not entrust it to the indifferent hands of others. Refuse to outsource your mind.

■

Lesson 81

Make the Case for Absolute Authority

> "The Russian Empire is so extensive that except for a sovereign master every other form of administration is harmful to it, for all the rest is slower in implementation and contains a great multitude of various passions which all tend to the fragmentation of central authority and power, than does a single sovereign who possesses all means for the curtailment of every kind of harm and considers the common good his own."
>
> ~Catherine, applying Montesquieu to Russia, June 1766

While Catherine wanted to bring an unprecedented degree of openness and even public participation into Russian government, she had no desire to sacrifice the finality of her absolute authority. Nevertheless, she was unwilling to assert her authority arbitrarily. Instead, she found in the works of the political philosopher Montesquieu the foundation for a rationale and justification for single-monarch absolute rule in Russia. For one thing, the empire was simply too vast to be ruled by more than one leader. A single central authority was essential to avoid fragmentation. Moreover, since a single leader can make decisions more quickly than a group of leaders, implementation of commands across the vast region would be simplified. This would also contribute to maintaining unity despite the wide separation of settlements and the ethnic diversity throughout the regions. In short, Catherine found an argument in favor of her power based on the good of the empire.

Whatever authority to which your position may theoretically entitle you, no one relishes arbitrary submission to command. The nature of your organization's hierarchy—even the law—may entitle you to authority, yet it is always most effective to embellish the basis of your leadership with reasons and principles that appeal to intellect, common sense, and a perception of the collective welfare of the enterprise. Never simply assume authority. Make an argument for it, and make it compelling.

■

Lesson 82
When Absolutely Necessary, Inject Your Authority

> "Yet if you notice in [the procurator of the War Collegium] needless timidity vis-à-vis [the head of the War Collegium], then give him to understand that you are speaking for me."
>
> ~Catherine, letter to her new procurator-general, Prince Aleksandr Vyazemsky, December 9, 1764

Catherine dispatched Prince Vyazemsky, whom she had appointed procurator-general (essentially supervisor of the Senate), to visit the procurator of the War Collegium (roughly, her secretary of war) to inform him that the members of the War Collegium were overstepping their authority by countermanding the order of provincial governors. She instructed Vyazemsky to point out that this was "in contradiction to [her] Personal decree" and further instructed him to remind the procurator "of his duty."

If Catherine's letter ended here, it would hardly be worth noting–except, perhaps, as an example of a manager issuing a clear, forceful instruction. But Catherine continued. She asked the prince to "read" this man. If he seemed to exhibit "needless timidity" as compared with the head of the War Collegium, who was actually his subordinate, then the prince was to emphasize that the order came from the empress.

This is an extraordinary insight into Catherine's management style. She wanted the empire's officials to exercise *their* authority to do *their* jobs. Only if they would not or could not do so effectively did she intervene. As for Prince Vyazemsky, she had no desire to compromise his authority by transforming him into a mere mouthpiece for her commands; however, if the procurator of the War Collegium seemed incapable of asserting his proper authority over a subordinate on instructions from a prince, she wanted Vyazemsky to "give him to understand" that the instructions came from Catherine. Thus, Catherine wielded her power with careful judgment and prudent economy.

Power is all too easily squandered. Throw your weight around, and you will soon blunt your command presence and, with it, your authority. Empower others to act with appropriate authority, so that you do not have to squander yours. Avoid casting your managers and supervisors in the role of messenger—a mere vessel to convey your orders—but when their authority is not sufficient to motivate an action, don't hesitate to deliver a full, undiluted shot of your direct authority.

■

Lesson 83

Beware the Lure of Despair

> "It is not surprising that Russia had many tyrants among her sovereigns. The nation is naturally restless, ungrateful, and filled with informers and men who under the pretext of zeal try to turn everything in their path to their own profit."
>
> ~Catherine, 1769, quoted in John T. Alexander, *Catherine the Great: Life and Legend*

Catherine assumed the Russian throne with eyes open to the formidable difficulties inherent in governing the nation. Nevertheless, she was determined to leave Russia better than she had found it, and, armed with the ideas and ideals of the Enlightenment, she was optimistic about her prospects. Throughout her long reign, circumstances seemed often to mock her optimism, and there were times when she yielded to pessimism. Late in her reign, with the specter of the French Revolution looming large, she even resorted to acts founded in the kind of tyranny she criticized in previous Russian monarchs.

Despair is a powerful lure, and even Catherine the Great sometimes succumbed. In remarking that the preponderance of tyrants among Russia's rulers was "not surprising," she did not welcome tyranny nor excuse it, but she did rationalize it, as if it were inevitable. She blamed the tyranny of tyrants on the nature of the Russian people, expressing an attitude—all too common among leaders—that is at best counterproductive and at worst downright destructive. At bottom, it is the proposition that change, in some places and in some circumstances, is impossible.

To despair of the possibility of change is to justify the old ways, even if they are manifestly the *bad* old ways. Resist despair, no matter how seductive.

Lesson 84
Build Big Ideas on Personal Observation

> "Visiting Moscow gave Catherine . . . ideas . . ."
>
> ~John T. Alexander, *Catherine the Great: Life and Legend*

Catherine was a great reader. Political and social theory engrossed her. She corresponded directly with the likes of Voltaire, Diderot, and Rousseau. She quickly evolved an ideology that some have called "democratic absolutism"–though it might be better described as *enlightened autocracy.*

Reading, theory, ideology: all were central in forming Catherine's vision for the Russian Empire. Nevertheless, she was hardly fixed to her desk. On the contrary, she was passionate about vigorous exercise in the outdoors and earned renown as a horsewoman. She was certainly no "theoretical" leader. Everyone who visited her court was impressed by her hands-on style of governance and her close attention to detail. And she was hardly an ideologue. Catherine had principles and ideals, but she was, above all, a pragmatist. More important, her most visionary goals grew directly out of personal observation of the reality in which she lived and through which she traveled.

Catherine made sweeping reforms in the economy and demographics of Russia. In a successful effort to control food prices, which were under pressure from the demands of war, she ordered prices in St. Petersburg to be comprehensively monitored twice a week, with reports delivered directly to her. She increased price competition by abolishing state grain monopolies, and she established grain storage facilities in major towns to moderate bread prices, which–as she knew–principally determined the cost of living for Russians.

In all big Russian cities, jammed with ramshackle wooden buildings, fire was a perpetual enemy. Catherine immediately provided funds to rebuild St. Petersburg's vital hemp warehouses after fire had destroyed them. Then she visited Moscow, where her direct observations gave her even bigger ideas about reshaping the urban centers of her country.

Moscow, she observed, was crammed with little factories and workshops, the existence of which promoted the development of squalid slums in their vicinity. On October 23, 1762, Catherine issued an edict banning the construction of new factories and workshops in badly overcrowded St. Petersburg and Moscow, directing that industrial expansion should take place in provincial towns, which not only had room for such facilities but also needed population. With these plans in place to relieve population pressures in the biggest cities, Catherine created a Commission for the Reconstruction in Masonry of Moscow and St. Petersburg, intending to transform both places from collections of wooden firetraps into relatively fireproof cities of brick and stone. Nor was she content merely to convert from one building material to another. She formed a comprehensive urban-planning agency to survey the capitals and prepare truly comprehensive plans for their ambitious reconfiguration. Her ultimate goal was to recast urban Russia into the mold of progressive Western Europe, thereby raising Russia to a level of civilization and sophistication on a par with such nations as Germany and France.

Catherine well understood that her vision would require many decades to realize. For her, this was all the more reason to make accurate personal observations now and to undertake specific projects immediately. Her most urgent concern was to improve the living conditions of urban Russians, to make them healthier, and to redistribute population from the two biggest cities to major towns in the hinterlands. She therefore used her own personal funds to finance public hospitals offering free treatment and to establish "foundling homes" to care for children whose parents were unmarried or indigent. At the same time, she accelerated incentives to build factories in smaller towns, thereby encouraging working-class residents of Moscow and St. Petersburg to move to them. Catherine also took steps, through the Senate, to encourage foreign immigration into Russia as well as to entice Russian refugees and émigrés to return. As part of this program, Catherine promised complete religious toleration—at least for Christians. During her reign, massive projects of social engineering and population resettlement—none of it forced, all of it conducted through positive incentives—reshaped and reinvigorated Russian society as well as Russian infrastructure. They were big ideas, but they all began with discrete, practical actions based directly on personal observation.

Business and political leaders often speak of a gulf between "theory" and "practice," as if it were some natural, inevitable, immutable, and unbridgeable separation. It need not be. The truly visionary leaders do not merely cross that gulf; they routinely eliminate it by refusing to formulate theories, ideas, and concepts in isolation from the reality they directly observe. What the twentieth-century American poet William Carlos Williams said about the root of true poetic expression can be applied equally to such productively imaginative managers: "No ideas but in things." As the best works of the literary imagination are ultimately rooted in closely observed reality, so the most profound entrepreneurial and institutional visions begin when a leader looks up, down, left, and right. This leader sees what works, what fails, and what could work better, and then formulates a plan to transform the present into the future.

■

Lesson 85

Offer Leadership under Law

> "It is better to be subject to the Laws under one Master, than to be subservient to many."
>
> ~Catherine, to the Russian Senate, 1767

Catherine ruled an empire that had long upheld the doctrines of absolute monarchy and autocratic governance. Nevertheless, Russia, like the rest of the world, was entering into an era of the Enlightenment, in which new models of government of, by, and for the people were challenging the status quo. Catherine herself borrowed much from the Enlightenment political philosophers Montesquieu, Rousseau, and Voltaire, among others. Yet, for all her progressive ideas, she was a confirmed autocrat. She had no intention of relinquishing authority to any other individual or governing body. She was, however, very willing to submit to the very same "Laws" to which the lowest of her subjects submitted. That is, while she asserted that the monarch's authority to administer the laws is absolute, she also pointed out that authority itself is subject to the laws and, therefore, not absolute, arbitrary, or tyrannical. In effect, this "absolute" monarch concluded a social contract with her subjects, which hardly made them equals, but it did unite them in the same enterprise–one in which "the Laws" were supreme.

As the leader of an enterprise, you are perfectly justified in establishing yourself as the ultimate authority, but you are not justified in asserting your authority arbitrarily or despotically. You, as boss, may make and administer the rules, but they are empty if they do not apply to you as they do to those who report to you. Submission to a rational system of rules unites an enterprise. It is a contract between those who lead and those who follow.

Lesson 86

Make Law Supreme

> "Political liberty does not consist in the notion that a man may do whatever he pleases; liberty is the right to do whatsoever the laws allow. . . . The equality of the citizens consists in that they should all be subject to the same laws."
>
> ~Catherine, *The Great Instruction,* 1767

Catherine sought to avoid both anarchy as well as the tyranny of arbitrary power. Her middle course between these two extremes was to embrace the supremacy of law. In this, her reasoning was that, if everyone were subject to the same laws, they would be equal. Only law can guarantee the equality of citizens as well as protect their liberties.

Heed the leading principle of Catherine's *Great Instruction* by formulating a practical set of rules, principles, and guidelines to be applied equally to every member of your organization. Subject everyone to the same set of rules. Allow freedom within the rules. In cases of dispute, resort first and last to *the rules* rather than to the conflicting arguments and differing opinions of the moment.

■

Lesson 87

See It with Your Own Eyes

> "Here I am in Asia: I wished to see it all with my own eyes."
>
> ~Catherine, letter to Voltaire, from Kazan, May 29, 1767

Having radically revised the Russian legal code, Catherine traveled throughout her empire to observe firsthand the effect of the laws and how they might be improved. Travel in the eighteenth century was arduous–even dangerous–but Catherine was determined to get direct, personal knowledge of her vast and diverse realm. She wrote to Voltaire that, in Kazan, were "twenty different peoples, which in no way resemble one another." Yet the government and the laws must serve everyone. "We have nevertheless to design a garment to fit them all." Catherine understood that it was relatively easy to come to agreement "on general principles," but, she asked, "what about the details? And what details!"

It is these, the "details," she could not entrust to the reports of others, but had to see with her own eyes, no matter how time-consuming, exhausting, and costly the journey.

> **The executive suite** is a comfortable, pleasant place—all the more reason to spend as little time in it as possible. Get out to every corner of your organization. Make personal contact with those who make up your enterprise. See what *they* see—for *yourself.* Understand their problems, challenges, and opportunities from *their* vantage point. Travel, visit, listen, observe.

■

Lesson 88

Reap the Reward beyond Success or Failure

> "[The work of the Legislative Commission] brought me light and knowledge from the whole empire, with which we had to deal and which we had to care for."
>
> ~Catherine, reflecting in 1794 on the often troublesome career of the Legislative Commission, quoted in John T. Alexander, *Catherine the Great: Life and Legend*

Catherine created a Legislative Commission of representatives from the major classes of the Russian people in order to secure guidance on the detailed execution of the principles laid down in her revision of Russian law called *The Great Instruction*. It was an unprecedented act for a Russian monarch and by any measure a noble experiment in government. Nevertheless, the commission often proved nonproductive, counterproductive, confused, argumentative, and generally burdensome. The institution failed to accomplish what it had been created to do: craft a body of specific, practical, and executable laws based on *The Great Instruction*. Indeed, the codification of Russian law would not be accomplished in any truly credible fashion until some forty years after Catherine's reign had come to an end.

Whatever the degree of her disappointment, Catherine did not regard her experience with the Legislative Commission as a failure. She did not deny that it had failed to achieve the task she had set for it, but she praised it as an institution that had given her the one reward that is beyond final success or failure. It brought her "light and knowledge," firsthand data from "the whole empire." This in itself was a contribution of inestimable value to her reign.

Business leaders gamble every day. Few ventures—perhaps none—are without risk. Few—perhaps none—come with a guarantee of specific, quantifiable gain. Yet within the inevitable and often inscrutable calculus of risk and reward, one class of venture is virtually a sure bet. Any project that, at the very least, promises a return of knowledge, insight, and understanding is a win. Its value is absolute.

■

Lesson 89
Define Responsibilities, Set Limits

> "1. The Senate cannot issue laws.
>
> "2. The old ones it can confirm.
>
> "3. The Senate ought to uphold, in a word, the laws. . . ."
>
> ~Catherine, instructions to Procurator-General Prince Vyazemsky, November or December 1767

Eager to define the responsibilities of the Senate as well as the limits of its authority, Catherine issued a set of clear directives to her procurator-general, the official charged with guiding the Senate. She began with three principles, culminating in the Senate's duty to uphold rather than make laws. From these general principles, she derived more specific guidelines. The most important of them was a prohibition against purporting to "explain the laws" by giving "them a meaning that is nowhere to be found in the words of the law." Among human beings in Russia, Catherine wanted there to be no mistake: Her authority was supreme. But she put even herself in a position subordinate to the rule of law, taking care to specify that the words of the laws were sacred, absolute, and not subject to reinterpretation at will.

The occasion of this communication to Prince Vyazemsky was the Senate's attempt to punish an entire village for the murder of a lord and his wife at the hands of their serfs. The Senate argued that the failure of the villagers to defend the lord and lady was the equivalent of murder, so that the villagers deserved the same punishment as the serfs who actually committed the bloody crime. In objecting to this proposal, Catherine explained that she endeavored "in all ways to distinguish crimes and punishments," whereas the "Senate confounds murder with non-defense of a lord and wishes that the murderers be equated with the non-defenders." She went on to explain that "there is a great difference between murder, knowledge of murder, and obstruction or non-obstruction to murder." She warned that if such willful reinterpretation of written law were permitted to stand, "if in response to and in punishment for the life of one lord whole hamlets will be destroyed," then "a riot of all bondaged hamlets will ensue . . . ."

Catherine believed that the absolute rule of law, set above the power of officials to willfully reinterpret it, was necessary–and not only to protect individuals. She saw consequences for the entire state and, indeed, for all humanity: "For if we do not agree to the diminution of cruelty and the amelioration of the intolerable position for the human species, then . . . Even against our will they [peasants and serfs] themselves will seize it [authority] sooner or later." Not only would this be a catastrophe for Russia, but also a failure of humanity.

Power tends to beget power, as those who have power generally use that power to seek and acquire yet more. To manage power, you, as the leader of the enterprise, must exercise your power to precisely define the responsibilities of each member of the organization as well as set clear and inviolable limits to the authority of each in carrying out their prescribed responsibilities. All of this must be put in writing, in the form of job descriptions that are rigorously adhered to.

The alternative to this system includes everything from misunderstandings to outright turf wars—a spectrum of consequences that is invariably destructive.

■

Lesson 90
Take Ownership of Action

> "Tell a thousand people to draft a letter, let them debate every phrase, and see how long it takes and what you get."
>
> ~Catherine, quoted in Robert K. Massie, *Catherine the Great: Portrait of a Woman*

It may be hard to imagine Catherine the Great meeting Harry S. Truman in some world beyond our own, but if the two ever did get to talking, we can make two assumptions: Both heads of state would have a lot to say about the nature of leadership and its responsibilities, and both would agree on the significance of the famous plaque the American president displayed on his Oval Office desk: "The Buck Stops Here."

Whatever else power is, it is primarily about taking ownership of action. This is both the greatest prerogative of a strong leader–and the heaviest burden.

To have the authority to take ownership of a problem, project, opportunity, or issue greatly facilitates action. Left to a thousand people, a decision may never be reached or, if reached, may be virtually unrecognizable as a decision at all. The decision of one empowered leader, however, may be made quickly and efficiently. It may also be ill-informed and create disaster. Nevertheless, timely action based on efficient decision-making has a better chance of success than inaction, tardy action, or total indecision. Such was Catherine's defense of absolute monarchy.

Demand that the buck stop with you, and understand that the prerogative of decision and action entails the burden of owning all the consequences. To pass the buck is to abandon the power, privilege, and responsibilities of leadership. Do this, and you relinquish leadership, whether or not you keep your job.

Lesson 91
Value an Affirmative Spirit

> "[Assess] the goodness of their hearts, the liveliness of their manners, the earnestness or joy of their attitude, the fearfulness or fearlessness in traveling and other important qualities of spirit."
>
> ~Catherine, instructions to her agents charged with assessing candidates for marriage to her son and heir, Paul, 1773, quoted in John T. Alexander, *Catherine the Great: Life and Legend*

There was nothing unusual about royal parents taking great care to ensure "a good match" for their offspring. Typically and traditionally, the criteria for evaluating marriage candidates were chiefly political and diplomatic. For Catherine, however, it was overwhelmingly a matter of character and attitude–what she called "spirit."

For Paul's bride, she sought a young woman with a good heart, lively manners, an earnest and joyful attitude, and a fearless spirit conducive to enduring (and even enjoying) travel–an activity, Catherine learned, that was essential to effective governance. All of her criteria for a bride were, not coincidentally, qualities she herself claimed to possess in abundance, with joy the most important of all.

Catherine believed in the creative power of an affirmative spirit. Possess a positive and optimistic attitude dominated by joy, in which fearlessness triumphs over fearfulness, and you are emotionally equipped to do great and productive things. To a remarkable degree, organizations form their collective attitude and their approach to business by emulating the person at the top. A CEO's personality is disseminated throughout the company. There is nothing to be gained by cynicism or pessimism, which, all too often, are mistaken for "prudence" or "realism." There is, on the contrary, everything to be gained by projecting enthusiasm, optimism, and joy. These are multipliers of collective energy, and they cost the organization exactly nothing.

■

Lesson 92
Be the Example

> "My objective was, through my example, to save from death the multitude of my subjects who, not knowing the value of this technique, frightened of it, were left in danger."
>
> ~Catherine, explanation of why she had undergone smallpox inoculation, written response to the Senate and Legislative Commission, November 20, 1768

Smallpox inoculation was introduced to the West by Lady Mary Wortley Montagu (1689–1762), who, as the wife of Edward Wortley Montagu, British ambassador to the Ottoman Empire, had seen it used in Turkey. Greatly impressed, she had her children inoculated (she herself bore the scars of having survived the disease in youth), and she brought the practice back to England in the 1720s. Inoculation spread fairly rapidly throughout Western Europe. Despite great controversy and significant danger of infection, it was regarded among the well-educated as a genuine medical advancement. Eastern Europeans, however, were far more reluctant to adopt the treatment.

Catherine studied the issue carefully and sought the advice of both Russian and Western European physicians. She reached the conclusion that inoculation was indeed effective and, while it had serious risks, they were risks well taken. Instead of merely urging her subjects to seek inoculation, she decided that the most effective form of persuasion she could adopt was her own example. She also presented Paul, her son and heir to the Russian throne, for inoculation.

Her personal example proved highly persuasive throughout Russia, beginning within her own court. A grateful Senate presented their formal thanks and awarded her twelve commemorative gold medals.

> **"Do as I say,** not as I do" is a familiar but cynical prescription for leadership. It may elicit some level of compliance, but it will never produce enthusiastic engagement with the actions and policies you promote. Nothing is more persuasive than putting skin in the game. Lead by example wherever and whenever possible.

■

Lesson 93
Do Not Worship Ancestral Beards

> "The condition of Moscow greatly disturbs me, for besides sickness and fires there is much stupidity there. All this recalls the beards of our ancestors."
>
> ~Catherine, letter to Nikita Panin, her privy counselor and political mentor, August 25, 1770

Russian cities–especially squalid, overcrowded, ramshackle Moscow–were frequently subject to the twin scourges of epidemic disease (smallpox, cholera, and even bubonic plague) and catastrophic fire. Catherine acted vigorously to address these problems. She embraced the modern–and, at the time, controversial–practice of smallpox inoculation, she worked to modernize Russian medicine and medical education, she funded foundling homes and hospitals dedicated to victims of venereal diseases (also rampant, especially in the cities), and she took large-scale action to tear down wooden Moscow and rebuild it as a city of stone and masonry.

Disease and fire were formidable foes, but, Catherine discovered, her most powerful enemy was "stupidity" founded on the mindless worship of past practices—what she called the "beards of our ancestors."

The weapons she employed to overcome self-destructive ancestor-worship were education, her own example as a learned reformer, and the importation of what we might call "best practices" from the more "advanced" states of Western Europe. Most of all, however, she worked to persuade her ministers as well as her subjects that all of the changes she proposed were aimed at *preserving* as well as *advancing* Russia. They were, she endeavored to demonstrate, intended to protect and further the best traditions of the Russian state and the Russian people. They were not innovations for the sake of innovation; rather, they were intended to guard and enhance Russian lives.

Instituting significant change is bound to make at least some members of an organization uncomfortable and resistant. Emulate Catherine by educating team members to the need and the benefits of whatever changes you propose. Set an enthusiastic personal example. Study and selectively borrow the "best practices" of other enterprises. In addition, think twice before you put the emphasis on the "change" part of *changes*. Emphasize the continuities between long-held principles and present objectives. For example, you might say, "I realize that these new procedures are going to take some getting used to, but I am convinced that they will help us achieve greater efficiency, which means a better bottom line. Some of the methods may be new, but the goal is what it has always been: products and prosperity we can be proud of."

Lesson 94
Try Delaying Tactics

> "It is necessary to be a Fabius, yet one's hands itch to thrash the Swede."
>
> ~Catherine, to her council concerning the attempts of Sweden's Gustav III to provoke war, June 20, 1788, quoted in John T. Alexander, *Catherine the Great: Life and Legend*

In 1772–much as Catherine herself had done against Peter III–Gustav of Sweden led a bloodless coup that put him on the Swedish throne, albeit without legal authority to declare war. This restriction gnawed at him because he believed that a short, sharp war was precisely what he needed to force his lingering opposition to declare their support for him. As Gustav rattled his saber, demanding the recall of the Russian ambassador, Catherine saw that he was preparing a possible assault on St. Petersburg. She prudently ordered the fortress of Kronstadt, just nineteen miles west of the city, reinforced and put on a war footing, and then she diverted a naval squadron from its Mediterranean-bound course to the seas off Reval.

Catherine did not want a war with Sweden, largely because she could see nothing enduring to gain from it. She briefly considered officially recognizing Gustav III's legitimacy on the Swedish throne, but quickly decided that such support would undermine her own standing. Therefore, ignoring her aggressive instincts–her "hands itch[ed] to thrash the Swede"–she called for defensive measures. Rather than launch a preemptive attack, Catherine thus emulated the example of Fabius, whose life she well knew from her study of Plutarch.

Roman politician and general Quintus Fabius Maximus Verrucosus richly deserved his famous agnomen (Roman nickname), *Cunctator*, ("delayer"). It was a reference to his successful use of delaying tactics against Hannibal during the Second Punic War, which lasted from 218 to 201 BCE. Keenly assessing the military superiority of the Carthaginians, Fabius resisted popular and political pressure to engage Hannibal in a showdown. Instead, he shadowed Hannibal's army and attacked supply chains while simultaneously avoiding pitched battle. By this delaying tactic, he managed (albeit at significant cost to the Roman Legion) to wear Hannibal down and force his withdrawal. Those who studied Roman history regarded Fabius as an object lesson in the potential value of delay, provided it worked hardship on one's foe while buying oneself time to improve a defensive position or other circumstance.

The hardest part about adopting the Fabian approach is resisting one's own urge to act quickly in the face of a perceived threat. Catherine possessed sufficient self-control to ignore this impulse. It was one thing to fight offensive campaigns in distant places, as she did against the Turks in the Crimea. But to risk defeat on the very doorstep of Russia's imperial city, St. Petersburg, would be foolhardy in the extreme–precisely the kind of thing her former husband would have done. The safer and surer way to victory was to wear down Gustav, whose popular support, she well knew, was severely limited. Rather than attempt to overcome the Swede's temporary military strength, Catherine decided to force Gustav to squander his resources in what she believed would be a time-consuming and futile assault.

In the heat of the moment, hasty action—more typically, *reaction*—is often more harmful than inaction. On the other hand, a passive failure to act is hardly desirable. Instead, consider buying time by employing deliberate delaying tactics. This "Fabian approach" can give you the advantage of additional time to formulate the best possible strategy, acquire more resources, and recruit allies—while compelling your opponent to spend *his* valuable resources. For example, when a competitor slashes the price of a product you also offer, your initial impulse will be to engage in a potentially costly price war. Sometimes, this is the best tactic—even if it means pricing merchandise below your own cost. An alternative, however, is to respond by offering more value, such as a "free" extended warranty, complementary installation, and so on. Such incentives may not quickly defeat your competition, but they might force him to prolong his reduced pricing policy until a breaking point is reached. In the long run, you end up with a superior offer, while your competition suffers a bad quarter.

■

Lesson 95
Fortify Your Soul

"It fortifies my soul."

~Catherine, on why she reads and rereads *Plutarch's Lives,* letter to her secretary Alexander Khrapovitsky, April 1790

Lives of the Noble Greeks and Romans, more familiarly called *Plutarch's Lives,* was Catherine's favorite book. Written by the Greek historian Plutarch (ca. 46–120 CE), this collection of paired biographies was intended to exhibit the moral virtues as well as vices of each of the most famous Greeks and Romans. Catherine found endless guidance in it. Reading about the careers of those who had made their mark upon the world long before she made hers gave the empress both insight and comfort. She felt less alone as a leader.

Reading *Plutarch's Lives* fortified her soul, and she resorted to it particularly in times of crisis, as when Sweden's Gustav III brought war to her very doorstep in St. Petersburg in the spring of

1790. She did not seek escape in her reading, but rather inspiration in the experience of those who had ruled before her.

Seek fresh inspiration and new energy wherever you can. Identify what nourishes your soul. Then work to find plenty of it. Indulge yourself in sources of encouragement.

■

Lesson 96

Offer a Brave Spirit

> "In Her Majesty the spirit of bravery is always present."
>
> ~Remark of Pyotr Zavadovsky, counselor, confidante, and favorite of Catherine, July 1788

Confronted in 1788 by an unwanted conflict with Sweden, Catherine skillfully deployed delaying tactics as she prepared for war. During this time, she discussed her fears and doubts with her inner circle, but she never betrayed these emotions to the larger government or the public. To the public, she projected nothing but supreme confidence–a "spirit of bravery," which was "always present" in her, as Zavadovsky described it.

Worry, doubt, and uncertainty are part of leadership. Let these motivate the kind of probing questions that should enter into high-stakes decision-making. Once you have reached a decision, however, the only statements to make and the only attitude to project are those growing out of a brave spirit. This is the most valuable feeling you can give your team, and the most effective way to create this feeling is to focus on the future: "The cutbacks will build a ready cash reserve that will position us to mount a dynamite promotional campaign early next year. Thanks to this, we can expect a spectacular launch. Next year will outperform this year. Count on it."

■

Lesson 97
Don't Lose the Mind Game

"I have listened to empty cannons for more than 25 years."

~Catherine, when asked if she heard the enemy's cannon, May 23, 1790, quoted in John T. Alexander, *Catherine the Great: Life and Legend*

For three days, Gustav III of Sweden unleashed a "terrific cannonade" within earshot of Tsarskoye Selo, the Russian imperial residence fifteen miles south of St. Petersburg. The physical damage was not great, but Gustav intended a severely wounding psychological effect. During the onslaught, he sent Catherine a message, asking if the chalices he had given in 1777 as a gift to Catherine were still unbroken and if she could hear his cannon from her imperial residence.

Catherine did not deign to reply to Gustav, but she did calmly respond to the court officials who were with her in Tsarskoye Selo with a question of her own: "Does he really think that I take chalices out of churches?" She followed this by casually remarking that she had been listening "to empty cannons for more than 25 years." The empress understood that Gustav was playing a mind game, and she did not intend to lose. Those who heard her were deeply impressed.

During the desperate World War II Battle of the Bulge at the end of 1944, when German forces surrounded the U.S. 101st Airborne Division, which was holding the strategically critical town of Bastogne, the Nazi commander sent officers under a white flag with a demand for surrender. The commanding officer of the 101st, Brigadier General Anthony McAuliffe—outnumbered and surrounded—responded to the demand with a single word: "Nuts!" He knew his situation was precarious, but he also knew that if he lost the mind game, losing the battle would follow. His justly celebrated monosyllabic reply—a masterpiece of defiantly dismissive American vernacular—demonstrated that he had no intention of losing either the mind game or the battle. In the most anxious days of the battle, McAuliffe's reply was published worldwide, giving heart to all those united against the Nazis. It lifted the morale of the Allied armies, which not only survived the battle, but won it, breaking the back of Hitler's final offensive.

You *may* lose any battle, but you *will* lose any battle in which you surrender before the fight actually commences.

■

The Builder

CATHARINE II. ALEXIEVNA. EMPRESS OF RUSSIA. REIGNED XXXV YEARS.

Lesson 98
Involve Yourself

"My lord, it is up to a sovereign to involve himself or not with the governing of his country. If he does not get involved, then the country governs itself, but it governs itself badly."

~Monsieur Pechlin, minister for Grand Duke Peter's duchy of Holstein, quoted in Catherine's *Memoirs,* 1759–1794

The Grand Duke Peter, Catherine's husband and heir to the Russian throne, had titular rule over Holstein, his native duchy, but neglected to govern it. When his minister for Holstein, a Monsieur Pechlin, had an audience with the grand duke in St. Petersburg, he scolded him–as deferentially as he possibly could–about his neglect of the duchy. Catherine recorded Pechlin's words and, many years later, reproduced them in her *Memoirs.* Clearly, they were important to her. They spoke of the difference between being a leader by position and title and being a leader by commitment and act. Catherine took her husband's bad example and Pechlin's words as a lesson in hands-on management. In contrast to Peter, she, as empress of Russia, would "involve" herself deeply in governing her country–in daily monitoring, analysis, adjustment, and governance, and for the long term, defining and enacting a vision for the empire.

Your position, job title, and job description mean nothing if you fail to enact the authority, responsibility, and stewardship they imply. A leader is defined strictly by the verb form of his or her title. That is, *a leader leads.*

Lesson 99
Be an Honest and Loyal Knight

> "If I may dare to use such terms, I take the liberty to assert on my own behalf that I was an honest and loyal knight . . ."
>
> ~Characterization of herself in her early days at the Russian court, recorded in her *Memoirs,* 1759–1794

Transplanted from the German hinterlands to the imperial court at the heart of the Russian Empire and matched with a grotesque monster–an overgrown boy–for a husband, Catherine dedicated herself to the daunting task of winning friends, allies, and supporters while neutralizing rivals and outright foes. Toward this end, she harnessed what she herself described as her naturally accommodating personality ("no one was ever with me a quarter of an hour without falling comfortably into conversation, chatting with me as if they had known me for a long time") and her natural "indulgence." Most of all, however, she endeavored to create the impression that "the strictest probity and goodwill were the impulses that [she] most readily obeyed."

Whereas some leaders strive to create respect, awe, and even fear, Catherine sought to instill trust. She was less interested in projecting command than service, and so she presented herself as "an honest and loyal knight." When the moment came for her to overthrow and replace her tragically inept husband as ruler of Russia, she had a foundation and network of supporters willing to trust her.

Leadership, especially in an enterprise dedicated to the common prosperity of all stakeholders, is not so much an issue of command as it is a project of service. Loyalty, integrity, honesty, and fearlessness—the qualities of a knight—are the qualities of a leader dedicated to serving his or her constituency. Cast yourself not in the role of monarch or czar, but rather in the role of a knight: ready, willing, and able to render bold, loyal, and effective service to the benefit of all.

■

Lesson 100

Focus on Value, Not Cost

> "These presents [gifts to create or to cement friendships] were the result of a fixed principle, of a natural prodigality and of a contempt for riches upon which I have always looked only as a means to procure for myself anything I liked."
>
> ~*Memoirs, 1759–1794*

The Empress Elizabeth would often criticize Grand Duchess Catherine for what she considered her spendthrift ways, and, when she ascended the throne, Catherine's spending became even more liberal. She made no apologies, in part ascribing her "contempt for riches" to a "natural prodigality" and in part to "fixed principle."

What was that principle? It was to use money to procure whatever she wanted. Most of the time, what she wanted was friendship and loyalty. Most of the money Catherine spent was spent on others, expressly for the purpose of starting, creating, nurturing, cementing, or repairing friendships. Catherine was less concerned about the monetary cost of these relationships than about the value her cash bought her. She did not *spend* money on her friends; rather, she *invested* in their friendship, the purchase of which represented great value to Catherine's survival, rise, and maintenance in power.

More often than not, leading a business enterprise comes down to making decisions about the allocation of money and other resources. Avoid thinking in terms of simple subtraction and instead frame these decisions as equations, in which cost is never considered apart from value gained. Cost is static; value, dynamic. Put the dynamic elements uppermost in any decision you make.

■

Lesson 101
Know When to Lead a Coup

> "Thus seeing that she had only two paths before her, that of sharing the misfortunes of a husband who hated her, who was incapable of following good advice, and who had no greater enemy than himself, or of saving the Empire, the Grand Duke's son, age seven, and herself, Catherine no longer hesitated, she saved that Empire."
>
> ~Catherine II, *Antidote,* 1770

On the face of it, Catherine II was a ruthless usurper. She led a coup d'état against her husband, Czar Peter III, after he had reigned a mere six months. Eight days later, Peter was dead, probably murdered by Aleksey Orlov, the younger brother of Grigory Orlov, one of Catherine's court favorites and a key conspirator in the coup. For his part, Aleksey wrote to Catherine that Peter had been killed in a drunken brawl with one of his jailers, and she, in turn, authorized a public announcement attributing the deposed czar's death to "haemorrhoidal colic." While many historians suspect Catherine's complicity in her husband's murder, none has ever produced evidence to support the charge.

No one knew better than Catherine herself the high-stakes gamble she took in leading the coup. Not only did she prove herself a disobedient wife, but she violated the very concepts of absolute rule and rule by divine right, which required the flawless appearance of legitimacy of authority. Assuming the throne by coup and usurpation hardly contributed to that appearance.

As Catherine explained, however, she saw but two paths before her. One was to cling to a husband who was, in truth, no husband–and not even a sane man. She wrote in the margin of her copy of the Abbe Denina's *Life and Reign of Frederick II* (1789) that Peter III "had no greater enemy than himself; all his actions bordered on insanity. . . . He took pleasure in beating men and animals." If she was therefore justified in feeling no fidelity to such a husband, neither was she under obligation to remain loyal to a monarch who was leading the empire to ruin. As she wrote in her *Memoirs*, the situation had become "a matter of perishing with [Peter III], or by him, or else saving myself, my children, and perhaps the state from the disaster that all this Prince's moral and physical faculties promised." Ultimately, the path she chose was to save herself, her children–including the heir to the throne–and the Russian Empire.

Convention always favors the status quo. The decision to depart from it, especially when the departure must be dramatic and extreme, is not to be taken lightly. But when it is clear that the status quo offers nothing but the illusion of safety and the reality of decline and doom, the time has come for a coup d'état. Change for the sake of change is a poor reason for change. Change for the sake of survival is better, and change for the purpose of saving and improving the enterprise is best of all. There is nothing inherently moral about the status quo.

Lesson 102
Lead the March

"She would lead this march herself."

~Robert K. Massie, *Catherine the Great: Portrait of a Woman*

Immediately after assuming the throne, Catherine resolved to consummate her coup d'état by causing the arrest of her deposed husband, Peter III. Loyal members of the elite Preobrazhensky Guards prepared to march to Oranienbaum to carry out the arrest. Seizing the moment, and determined to finish what she herself had begun, Catherine declared that *she* would lead the march personally. As sovereign, she knew she had the right to claim the colonelship of the Preobrazhensky Guards. She did so now, and she quickly borrowed portions of the regimental uniform and accoutrements from various Guards officers–the final piece, an ornamental sword knot, being handed to her by none other than Grigory Potemkin, marking her first meeting with the remarkable man who would become her top adviser, top general, and greatest love.

Thus arrayed, Catherine mounted a magnificent white stallion at ten in the evening, rode to the head of the Guards, and led a total of fourteen thousand Russian soldiers out of St. Petersburg and toward Oranienbaum. Not since England's Elizabeth I journeyed to Tilbury, Essex, on August 8, 1588, to inspect and inspirit the army charged with repelling an invasion by the Spanish Armada, had an empress made such a spectacular martial demonstration.

If you claim to be a leader, put yourself upfront. And make sure absolutely everyone sees you.

■

Lesson 103
Sell Selflessness

> "You see–it's not I who is acting; I only obey the people's wish."
>
> ~Catherine, quoted in Claude C. de Rulhiere, *A History or Anecdotes of the Revolution in Russia, in the Year 1762*

As Catherine, having led three regiments of Preobrazhensky Guards, rode up to the Peterhof at Oranienbaum to arrest Peter III, whom she had already overthrown, his chancellor, Mikhail Vorontsov, pleaded with her not to take up arms against a man who was both her czar and her husband. To this, Catherine calmly responded by dismounting from her white stallion and leading him onto a balcony of the palace. From here, she gestured toward the cheering crowd below.

"Deliver your message to them, sir. It is they who command here. I only obey."

It was the message with which she began her coup and with which she now consummated. In years to come, she would repeat it often: "I owe my accession to God and the will of the people." Most immediately, however, Vorontsov was thoroughly persuaded, and from that moment forward, he led other high officials in the fallen government of Peter III in submission to her.

Catherine's persuasive demonstration of selflessness moved all the main figures of the old government to accept and embrace her. It was a brilliant moment in this eighteenth-century Russian revolution.

Sell necessity, inevitability, and service to others. Offer compelling proof of selflessness. Assume full responsibility for your leadership decisions, but indelibly brand yourself as the servant of those you lead. If you cannot always be a servant leader, at least make yourself always appear as one.

Then step back and let everyone decide whether allegiance to an individual who promises to put their collective interest above all else is a good idea. This is the most effective sequence for leading profound change.

■

Lesson 104
Be Transparent

> "Catherine waved and smiled to the crowd as she arrived at the Winter Palace . . ."
>
> ~John T. Alexander, *Catherine the Great: Life and Legend*

Catherine II ascended the Russian imperial throne by overthrowing the sitting czar, who also happened to be her husband. Ordinarily, we would expect this to be at the very least a suspect act–furtive, carried out behind closed doors–and certainly not an occasion for smiles and waves. But Catherine made it public. As for those closed doors, she ordered the palace open to anyone who wanted to see her. From time to time, on that first day of her ascension, she lifted her newborn son Paul, the heir to the throne, in her arms and displayed him from the palace balcony to the cheering crowds below.

Catherine became empress by coup d'état, but she branded the event as a joyous occasion, transparent to all–an event in which the people of Russia were given a role and a stake. While Peter III's six-month reign had been too brief to be judged truly disastrous, he had begun by giving back hard-won territory to Prussia, and already his aloof contempt for the Russian people had become apparent. For her part, Catherine hardly mentioned the deposed czar, but, in a manifesto she published upon ascending the throne, she made it clear that she intended to rescue Russia from a one-sided and humiliating alliance with Prussia and to rescue Orthodoxy, the empire's sacred religion, from ruin at the hands of German Protestants. She presented her ascension as a joyous *public* occasion in which her "loyal subjects" had achieved salvation. From start to finish, Catherine made a point to explain her decisions and her rise to power as a victory for the people. Both she and the czar-husband she dumped were quite incidental to the welfare of Russia and the Russians.

Perception is reality, so clearly explain the reasons behind every endeavor to the employees of your enterprise. Decisions shrouded in secrecy or evasion only arouse suspicion and threaten the trust that sustains leadership. Make your intentions clear, and your "subjects" are more likely to buy into your vision.

■

Lesson 105

Answer Why

> "We were compelled . . . to mount our all-Russian sovereign throne . . ."
>
> ~Catherine, manifesto promulgated on the overthrow of Czar Peter III

A monarch bold enough to seize the throne might think it beneath her office and dignity to offer to her people a justification for the seizure. Catherine did not feel this way. Following the coup d'état, she issued a manifesto that answered, simply, straightforwardly, and compellingly, why she had made so bold at to overthrow her husband. The one-sided alliance he had concluded with Prussia, she argued, enslaved Russia, undermined all of the empire's institutions, and endangered Orthodoxy by bowing to Lutheranism. "Therefore," she wrote, "being convinced of such danger to our loyal subjects, We were compelled, accepting God and His justice as assistance, and especially seeing the clear and unfeigned desire of all our loyal subjects, to mount our all-Russian sovereign throne, wherein all our loyal subjects have solemnly given us the oath."

Why did Catherine ascend the throne? To save Russia and its "loyal subjects."

As she presented it, her action was not motivated by her own personal desire, but, rather, was something "compelled" and facilitated by "God and His justice" as well as by the will of the people themselves. As proof of her motive, she demonstrated her willingness to justify her actions to her people.

> **Those you lead**—those you serve—have only one question for you: *What will you do for me?* Frame all of your explanations and justifications for the actions you take as an answer to this question.

■

Lesson 106

Don't *Always* Make It Personal

> "You only did your duty."
>
> ~Catherine, to Field Marshal Münnich, August 1762

Catherine would have instantly understood the leading theme of Abraham Lincoln's 1865 Second Inaugural Address–the part about "with malice toward none, with charity for all" and the president's intention "to bind up the nation's wounds." Having overthrown Peter III, she had no desire to take vengeance on those who had served him loyally, provided they now dedicated themselves to her service. Thus she retained many of Peter's highest-ranking officials, among whom was the eighty-year-old Field Marshal Münnich, who (Catherine knew) had asked Peter to put him at the head of force that would march against St. Petersburg and retake the throne *from her.* However, Catherine understood that Münnich had intended nothing personal against her.

"You only did your duty," she assured him. Having won the war, Catherine immediately took steps to avoid losing the peace.

It can save you a lot of anguish and energy if you carefully distinguish business motives from personal ones. Each executive (including you) has a duty to the business he or she leads. Acknowledge this, and behave toward your competitors and colleagues accordingly. The world of business, especially within a given territory or industry, is remarkably small. Think hard before you decide to take anything personally.

■

Lesson 107

Embrace Chaos as Opportunity

> "Catherine . . . painted[ed] in somber hues the critical situation she inherited after her coup: an empty treasury, the army in Prussia unpaid for months, no credit abroad, huge state debts, thousands of peasants and workers on strike or in revolt, rampant ignorance and incompetence among officialdom–in short, utter chaos and near paralysis of government."
>
> ~John T. Alexander, *Catherine the Great: Life and Legend*

Deep into her reign, Catherine the Great delighted in recounting the condition in which she found Russia when she assumed its throne. Both Empress Elizabeth and, after her, the incompetent Peter III, had led the empire to the point of financial, administrative, diplomatic, social, and military collapse. It was chaos, and Catherine embraced it as an opportunity for greatness.

Embrace chaos, and do so with gratitude. It is to the leader of any enterprise what marble is to a sculptor: material as unyielding and difficult to work with as it is full of potential. Chaos exists to be ordered, tamed, and shaped. And that is what leaders do.

■

Lesson 108

Educate

General Plan for the Education of Young People of Both Sexes

~Title of a book by Empress Catherine II, published in 1764

In her determination to reform the administration of Russian government, Catherine II concluded that the nation required a corps of far more qualified civil servants than it had when she took the throne. This insight led her even further. The empress decided that the nation needed a more qualified citizenry, composed of people who possessed the education that would enable them to be genuinely useful to the empire. She therefore called on Ivan Ivanovich Betskoy, who served her in the somewhat vague capacity of personal secretary, to become her adviser on education. Placed in this position, he excelled, earning a place in history as an educational reformer and the man who implemented the first unified system of public education in Russia.

Specifics of the plan for Russian public education were set out in the book Betskoy wrote in collaboration with Catherine II. *General Plan for the Education of Young People of Both Sexes,* published in 1764, was a groundbreaking volume, founded on the pedagogical and developmental theories of John Locke and Jean-Jacques Rousseau, but insightfully adapted to the special circumstances of Russia.

As the years of her reign went by, Catherine continued to think and write about education. In 1781, she composed a Russian primer to teach reading, which became a bestseller in Russia and was the very first work of Russian literature to be translated into English. At this time, she also wrote the first original works of Russian children's literature, which were translated into German, French, and English. (She extracted one of these tales and adapted it into an opera libretto in 1786.) In 1783 and 1784, Catherine wrote *Notes Concerning Russian History* as a textbook for use in Russian schools, and in 1784 she composed *Instructions to Prince Nikolai Ivanovich Saltykov on the Upbringing of the Grand Princes,* a book-length treatise prescribing in detail an education program for her grandsons. Her culminating achievement was the drafting of *Statute of National Schools* in 1786, which was based on the *General Plan.*

Whether you make submarines or shoes, your business is only as good as the people who comprise it. Employees are—as it has often been pointed out, correctly—the greatest asset of any enterprise, even though they walk into the shop in the morning and out of it at night. Acquire, build, and develop this asset. Invest in education and training. You can make minor adjustments to your organization through statements of policy, the acquisition of new machinery, perhaps even the building of new facilities. But to truly transform your business, you must educate the people who *are* the business.

Lesson 109
Take Control

> "Asked whether she would review ambassadorial reports in full or, like previous sovereigns, only in extracts, she demanded the complete dispatches."
>
> ~John T. Alexander, *Catherine the Great: Life and Legend*

Before Catherine, Russian rulers–with the notable exception of Peter the Great–took very much a hands-off approach to foreign affairs. In part, this was in keeping with their desire to maintain what might be called Russia's "splendid isolation" among nations, but it also reflected an attitude that the Russian czar was a ruler far above the details. Moreover, a czar did not deign to negotiate, even with other sovereigns. For this reason, foreign policy was left to ministers and surrogates.

As Catherine saw it, this approach was counterproductive on three counts. First, Russia could no longer afford a policy of isolation. For the economic, military, and cultural good of the empire, Russia needed to be a part of Europe. Only in this way, Catherine believed, could the nation claim its rightful place in history. She saw this new orientation toward the West as the valuable legacy of Peter the Great, and she correctly believed that his legacy was in danger of being lost. She was therefore determined to build on it and develop it further, in ways that would ensure Russia's participation in the greater world stage.

Second, Catherine believed that to the degree that she remained aloof from foreign policy and was content to receive it second-hand from ministers, she would never reach maturity as the leader of the empire. The authority to govern was not merely the product of an official position and label, nor was it the consequence of popular acclamation. In Catherine's mind, the authority to govern was the outcome of taking direct and personal responsibility, of guiding and representing the nation–not only to one's own people, but to the rest of the world.

Finally, Catherine believed that no one in her court was more capable of managing foreign policy than she, and she always elevated the best people to the most critical positions.

In practical terms, Catherine proclaimed her intention to take personal control of foreign policy by immediately dissolving the position of chancellor of foreign affairs when she ascended the throne. For guidance, she turned less to living advisers than she did to the military and cultural legacy of Peter the Great. Moreover, she ensured that the rest of her court administration was aligned behind her decision. Not only did she dispense with the foreign affairs chancellor, but she also totally centralized the financial administration of the empire. She controlled the purse strings, and she put into place a mechanism that would allow budgetary planning to be sufficiently fluid so as to allow her to instantly back any war-making decisions with sufficient cash to go to war. In contrast to many of her predecessors, Catherine was not reluctant to accumulate and manage a national debt. She was less interested in hoarding assets than she was in making a place for Russia in the world.

Under Catherine the Great, Russia maintained a powerful alliance with Prussia, even though she used the slavishly Prussophile policy of her husband, Peter III, as a rationale to overthrow him in the coup of 1762. Under Catherine, Russia and Prussia would be equal partners in international affairs, not subordinate and master. She was an expansionist, winning substantial territories in two costly wars against Turkey in 1768 through 1774 and again in 1787 through 1791. She added Walachia and Moldavia in 1770 through 1774 and the Crimea, with its all-important access to the Black Sea, in 1783. She used this acquisition to vastly expand in the South what Peter the Great had begun on the Baltic Sea in the North. Once in possession of a Black Sea port, she built a great Russian naval fleet. Moreover, from her position of victory, Catherine led the three partitions of Poland in 1772, 1792, and 1795, carving up and sharing out the country with her allies while she gathered up conquests in Ukraine, White Russia, and Lithuania.

The objective of all this territorial expansion was the expansion of a great agricultural economy. She liberally rewarded her officers and troops with large grants of land, along with the serfs to work it. In this way, she "Russianized" the acquired territories and added to the wealth of the empire. All of it–from policy to conquest–emanated from her vision and her control of that vision's execution.

No word in the modern lexicon of business leadership is dirtier than *micromanagement*, and it is certainly true that the sight of many a forest has been lost on account of preoccupation with individual trees. We are suspicious of CEOs who demand direct control of logistical details. Yet the tendency of modern management theory has been to stress structures and systems that promote delegation, often at the expense of grappling with the basic issues of leadership, which involve personality, character, vision, and what military leaders would call "command presence." Catherine II was not a micromanager, but she did approach leadership by first defining her vision and its objectives, then determining what aspects of governance she needed to control directly and personally in order to ensure the prompt and complete implementation and realization of her vision.

These are steps every successful leader of enterprise must take. First, create a personal vision. Then, decide what is needed for its realization, and, having made these decisions, take personal and direct control of precisely those mechanisms necessary to execution, implementation, and ongoing management of your vision and its effects.

■

Lesson 110
Be Incredibly Generous

> "Catherine did not forget her friends."
>
> ~John T. Alexander, *Catherine the Great: Life and Legend*

Catherine II did not just give quid pro quo for services rendered to her, and, in contrast to Empress Elizabeth, she did not merely bestow cheap token gifts to acknowledge gratitude. Catherine did not forget her friends and supporters, on whom she showered rewards with extravagant generosity. For Grigory Orlov, who might be described as the architect of the coup d'état that put her on the throne, she set aside 50,000 rubles. Among forty other coup leaders, she immediately distributed 526,000 rubles and 18,000 male serfs. The cash value of this award easily exceeded 1 million rubles. Put this into the context of a state whose annual total budget amounted to 16 million rubles, and you can appreciate the magnitude of the gifts.

After the forty principal coup conspirators, the next level of top "stalwarts" received perpetual pensions of 5,000 rubles a year. Those in the tier below them were given either 800 serfs or 24,000 rubles each. Below this, the award was 600 serfs or 18,000 rubles. Nor did Catherine neglect the rank-and-file soldiers of the St. Petersburg garrison, each of whom was granted a half-year's salary–awards that totaled 225,890 rubles. To ordinary Russians, she was also generous. On a visit to Moscow, she carried with her 120 oak barrels packed with silver coins for general distribution (total cost: 600,000 rubles).

Catherine's purpose was not so much to buy friendship and bribe influential people (although this was unmistakably *part* of her intention) as it was to portray herself as an abundant font of generosity and the capacious source of all that was good and desirable. Her extravagance sent a powerful and powerfully effective message.

If you want to shape others' perception of you, make gestures of open-hearted, unfeigned, and unstinting generosity. It is an investment typically repaid to you many times over.

■

Lesson 111
Know Thyself

> "In 1768 she ordered the Academy of Sciences to make expeditions, reports, illustrations, and maps in a survey of Russia."
>
> ~Markus Cruse and Hilde Hoogenboom,
> "Introduction," *Memoirs of Catherine the Great*

While Catherine the Great expanded Russia into Asia Minor and Europe, and while she reached out to Western Europe's cultural luminaries, philosophers, artists, writers, and arbiters of taste–in the process purchasing the libraries of Diderot and Voltaire and amassing one of the world's greatest collections of European art–she also looked inward, to Russia itself. She quickly realized that none of her predecessors had ever surveyed, catalogued, and studied the "content" of the vast nation. If Russia was largely unknown to the world, it was also largely unknown to itself–and certainly to the Russian rulers who had preceded Catherine. The empress acted to remedy this great deficiency. In 1768, she commissioned an unprecedented series of expeditions into the heart of the vast empire. The project was akin to what U.S. president Thomas Jefferson would authorize Lewis and Clark to undertake in North America from 1804 to 1806, except that it involved larger forces and was better funded. Catherine assigned the Academy explorers to make full reports, to illustrate them graphically, and, above all, to map the great vastness of Russia in detail. Ultimately, these expeditions resulted in a monumental Russian atlas and, at a time when European interest in linguistics was proliferating, a comparative dictionary of the languages spoken in the Russian Empire. The project inspired Catherine to write essays on Russian history, seeking to take over from disparaging French interpreters and demeaning cultural critics Russia's national narrative. She personally sponsored and subsidized posthumous publication of *History of Russia from the Earliest Times* (1768) by Vasily Tatishchev (1686–1750), along with more than eighty other works of Russian history.

Most of us think of "vision" as a looking outward. Indeed, any leader must do this, but creating an accurate and useful picture of your company's context, current position, and future also requires looking within. Take every step necessary to know who you are as an organization, including your strengths, your weaknesses, your challenges, and your opportunities. Compile this data firsthand. Do not rely on received wisdom, tradition, and vague recollections, all of which tend quickly to crystallize into misleading mythologies and unquestioned assumptions.

■

Lesson 112
Kick Butt

> "Listen, Perfil'evich, if by the end of this week you do not bring me the instructions for the governors' duties, the manifesto against extortionists and Beket'ev's affairs completely finished, then I shall say there is no lazybones in the world like you, and that nobody with so many matters entrusted to him drags them out, as you do."
>
> ~Catherine II, message to her cabinet secretary, Ivan Perfilevich Elagin, spring 1764, quoted in John T. Alexander, *Catherine the Great: Life and Legend*

While the Russian czars enjoyed absolute power, the traditional administrative apparatus of Russian government was so inefficient that the czars themselves were held hostage to the prevailing incompetence of their own cabinets, ministers, and staff.

Such was the status quo. But Catherine was having none of it.

She drew up an ironclad schedule of regular eight A.M. meetings with her top ministers: one man on Mondays and Wednesdays, another on Tuesdays and Thursdays, and a third on Fridays and Saturdays. This regularity of communication with those who initiated the execution and implementation of her orders throughout the departments of government was a big step, but Catherine saw it as only the beginning. She rode herd on her ministers, never hesitating to give them a swift boot to the backside when she believed it necessary. There were no dire threats, just expressions of displeasure and a willingness to wield the heavy stick of shame. Catherine never hesitated to express her disappointment in personal terms, always with an edge of good-natured scolding–but with an edge, nonetheless. Presented this way, her orders compelled compliance from highly placed men who were loath, as it were, to experience another verbal jibe.

Handing out abuse is neither an effective nor a sustainable leadership tactic. But leveling with those who report to you, expressing (as appropriate) disappointment or delight in personal terms, can be a powerful motivator. Objective metrics—money, time, materials consumed, products produced—are indispensable to business. It is also important to remember that the bottom line is not exclusively about numbers. Business is conducted by people, and personal contact—one-on-one, face-to-face, and even (figuratively!) shoe-to-butt—can be potently motivating, facilitative, and even inspiring.

■

Lesson 113

Make Time to Manage Time

> "It was ordered to spend the first days in formalities, whereas now they are using for that those days in which they could have already begun to work."
>
> ~Catherine, directing her procurator-general to prod the Legislative Commission to use time productively, October 1767

Catherine convened a great Legislative Commission to proceed with the formulation and enactment of laws pursuant to the program she had laid down in her treatise, *The Great Instruction*. When she was told that a key subcommittee of the commission, the subcommittee on towns, had summarily adjourned to await the binding of copies of *The Great Instruction* Catherine flew into a rage.

"Have they really lost those copies which they already received as deputies in Moscow?" she asked Prince Vyazemsky, her procurator-general. She concluded that the adjournment was "evident laziness" as well as a "violation of the Procedures" she herself had established for the Legislative Commission. She pointed out to the prince that "it was ordered to spend the first days in formalities." Now, she complained, the subcommittee, by idling, would be using *work* days to arrange those formalities. The subcommittee had already fallen behind. Accordingly, she directed Prince Vyazemsky to order the "Directing Commission" to "respectfully" inform the subcommittee on towns that it was wasting time and was already dilatory.

Catherine enjoyed great wealth, and she spent freely. Even she understood, however, that one asset was absolutely finite and limited. She could not afford to squander time, and she could not tolerate any institution of her government to do so.

Catherine pressed everyone and every department in her administration to manage their time productively. She saw idling as the one waste of resources that could not be made up, and so she continually pushed for accountability.

As a manager, you must obtain and allocate numerous resources, including funds, supplies, and personnel. Managing these is difficult enough, but most demanding of all is the task of managing time. Of all your resources, time is the only one that is absolutely finite and nonrenewable. In the deepest and most basic sense of the word, time is precious. It therefore represents your top management priority.

■

Lesson 114
Take Care of Business

> "Her application to business is incredible. The welfare and prosperity of her subjects, the glory of her empire, are always present to her; and to all appearance her care will raise the reputation and power of Russia to a point which, at present, they have never reached . . ."
>
> ~Lord Buckingham, British envoy to Russia, 1763

Catherine II not only put in long hours, but also devoted the whole of her concentration to the business of her empire, including the welfare of her subjects and the "glory" of the realm. This latter consideration included growing the empire by expanding its boundaries, defending the empire from foreign enemies, and, perhaps most of all, raising both the reputation and power of Russia within the family of nations.

Catherine was intent on building, rebuilding, and generally rehabilitating the Russian "brand." To this end, she imported the best of Enlightenment culture and ideas, reformed Russian law, expanded Russian trade, and rewrote Russian history, reclaiming it from the German and French pens, which had not painted a flattering or productive picture of the Russian nation and people.

It is never healthy, neither physically nor emotionally, to wholly identify yourself with your enterprise. The ego needs its own space. This said, when you turn to business, turn to it with your whole mind and your whole heart. Focus on it. Bring to it all of your energy and presence. The greatest lesson of dynamic leaders like Catherine II is their willingness and ability to devote themselves to the business of leadership, exclusively, when such concentration is necessary. This is called taking care of business.

Lesson 115
Reform or Exclude Idlers

> "I have no need for idlers."
>
> ~Catherine, to Field Marshal Cyril Razumovsky's adjutant, regarding Field Marshal Buterlin's inattention to his military duties

In large measure, Catherine had the army to thank for the success of the coup d'état that had put her on the throne. Endeavoring to return the loyalty the military had shown her, she lavished funding on it, praised it, and gave officers at every level of command generous rewards. She drew the line, however, when it came to officers who failed to pull their weight. One such was Field Marshal Alexander Buturlin. He had achieved his senior command under the Empress Elizabeth and, during the Seven Years' War (1756–1763), even achieved overall command of Russian armies fighting in Prussia. All of this, however, was due more to Elizabeth's sponsorship than Buturlin's military prowess. Even by the 1750s, he had earned a reputation as a drunkard. By the time Catherine came to the throne, he was drinking more, passing his time at cards, and rarely attending to his military duties.

Catherine was infuriated by Buturlin's bibulous sloth and doddering incompetence, but she was loath to insult the army by summarily removing one of its most senior officers. Instead, she took aside one Elagin, the adjutant of another field marshal and Buturlin's brother-in-law. Then she asked him to convey–in her name–a strong message to Buturlin: that he should pay less attention to card games and more attention to his military duties. Then she added a warning: "I have no need for idlers."

The only standard by which you should evaluate each member of your team is by the extent to which the member contributes to the team. If possible, measure the contribution by some objective metric. Money is usually best because nothing is more objective than a number: revenue created, profits created, costs reduced, productivity increased, and so on. When you discover an underperforming team member, you have a choice.

First: You can do nothing, which is both easy and destructive. Not only does an "idler" represent a dead salary, but his or her presence typically creates resentment among other team members and thereby erodes morale—and, with it, efficiency and productivity.

Second: You can fire the underperformer. If you judge the team member to be hopeless, this may be the most effective course—not only for your team, but for the underperformer, who may well be better suited to working in another environment.

But you should not be too hasty to take so final a step. Generally, the most desirable course—the option that promises the most for the team and for the individual in question—is to reform the "idler" by converting him or her into a producer. By taking the time to work with an underperformer, you demonstrate that you value him or her. Very often, this alone is sufficient to stimulate the extra effort required to improve performance dramatically. It creates a motivation built both on accepting a challenge and wanting to please you because you have shown compassion and loyalty. Reformed "idlers" often make highly motivated employees.

■

Lesson 116
Forget No One

> "Do not forget to make institutions about hospitals in the provinces as well, and submit them to Us."
>
> ~Catherine, instructions to the Medical Collegium, June 1764

Catherine set about reforming the practice of medicine in Russia by taking steps to increase the number of doctors in the empire, particularly Russian-born and Russian-trained doctors, and to raise the level of medical and apothecary care. She ordered the Medical Collegium, the empire's central medical authority, to assign a physician to each province and to cooperate with Moscow University to create a program that would increase the number of Russian (or at least Slavic) physicians serving the country. Catherine endowed the Medical Collegium with the authority to grant medical degrees based on the results of the examination of candidates. This required her to overcome objections from the collegium itself, whose members believed that physicians should receive first-class training at foreign universities instead of second-rate Russian degrees. Her response was to fund the improvement of medical training in Russia, so that it could produce physicians of the first rank.

In this effort, the tendency was to focus on the great urban centers of Moscow and St. Petersburg. The vision of Peter the Great, who reigned from 1682 to 1696, was to lift Russia by Europeanizing it. However, in this effort, he focused almost exclusively on the urban centers and, in particular, on St. Petersburg, which he himself had built. Catherine revered Peter–and would commission the French sculptor Étienne-Maurice Falconet to create a heroic equestrian monument to him in St. Petersburg–but she also believed that his vision for the nation had been incomplete because it focused on the city he called his "window on the West" and largely ignored the provinces. Catherine intended to forget no one, to leave no region out of her visionary plans. She ordered the Medical Collegium to "make institutions" (plans and charters) for hospitals to be built or improved in the provinces as well as in the capitals. Moreover, she insisted that such plans be sent directly to her for review and approval.

More destructive than failing to develop your enterprise is to improve one aspect of it—one department, one function—at the expense of others. Neglect any portion of your organization, and you risk introducing not only inefficiencies that will undo any improvements you make, but also resentment that jeopardizes overall morale. It is not wise to allow any member of a team or department of a company to feel relegated to the bench. Forget no one.

■

Lesson 117
Decree Transparency

> "I hope . . . that with God's aid we shall prevail [against the Pugachev Rebellion], for this riffraff has on its side neither order nor art; it is a rabble of miscreants who have at their head a deceiver as brazen as he is ignorant. Probably it will all end on the gallows but what sort of expectation is that for me, Mr. Governor, who has no love for the gallows? European opinion will relegate us to the time of Tsar Ivan the Terrible! That is the honor we must expect from this contemptible escapade. I have ordered that no further secret be made of this occurrence [the rebellion], because it is beneficial that substantial people should voice their opinions about it and speak of it in the desired spirit."
>
> ~Catherine, to the governor of Novgorod, December 1773

When Yemelyan Pugachev, a disaffected Russian army officer, led a rebellion among Cossacks in an attempt to overthrow Catherine in the name of the deposed–and deceased–Peter III, Catherine initially responded with measures to prevent word of the revolt from spreading. She hoped that secrecy would provide a screen behind which she could put down the rebellion before it was generally noticed. The Battle of Kazan, July 12 through 15, 1774, which resulted in a rebel sack of that city (in present-day Tartarstan, Russia), made further secrecy all but impossible. As Catherine now saw it, further secrecy was counterproductive, even destructive. She now called for frank transparency concerning what history variously calls Pugachev's Rebellion or the Cossack Revolt.

In a letter to the governor of Novgorod, Catherine explained that the entire rebellion would probably culminate in the mass execution of the rebels. For her, however, this was no victory. She had "no love for the gallows," she explained to the governor, because it would turn Western European opinion, which she had labored for so long to cultivate favorably, against Russia. Instead of an empire making strides toward entry into the family of Enlightenment nations, Russia would be relegated to the brutal era of Ivan the Terrible. She understood that she could not counter this perception with secrecy. Secrecy is the absence of information, and, in that absence, people, monarchs, and nations create their own versions of reality, typically exaggerating the worst.

But she also understood that she could not shape the world's perceptions with mere propaganda. Hollow assertions would not be believed–and, again, everyone would assume the very worst. The only effective course was one of transparency, in which "substantial people should voice their opinions" and speak of the rebellion in what Catherine believed was "the desired spirit." Given license to talk, she believed that the Russian people themselves would reveal Pugachev to the Western world as "a deceiver as brazen as he is ignorant." In this context, Catherine's own effort to put down the rebellion would be seen as thoroughly justified.

What could speak more clearly than transparency? In the absence of credible information from sources perceived as honest, the world will create its own narratives about you, your motives, and the intentions of your organization. Unclench your fists. Open your books.

■

Lesson 118

Play Favorites

> "Nothing can more clearly prove the strength of mind which the Imperial Catherine possesses, than her conduct toward her favourites. . . ."
>
> ~ *The Daily Universal Register* (predecessor to *The Times* of London), July 1787

In her own day as well as in the eyes of history, Catherine was famous–perhaps infamous–for cultivating a system of "favorites"–courtiers upon whom she lavished gifts of cash, estates, serfs, and other forms of preferment. By 1795, the penultimate year of her reign, she had spent 10.6 million rubles on her favorites, some 13.5 percent of Russian state expenditures.

In her own day–as well as in much modern lore about her–the favorites were all assumed to be Catherine's lovers. It was universally believed that she had the insatiable sexual appetite of a nymphomaniac. In fact, most historians agree that she had "just" twelve lovers during her long reign, some of whom (but not all) were also her favorites. Although favoritism was effectively institutionalized in her court, as well as that of Elizabeth before her, the role of favorite was by no means a formal political office. Nevertheless, most authorities count twice as many clear favorites as known lovers (not all of whom were favorites) in Catherine's court. Thus, for Catherine, the institution of favorites served a primarily nonromantic purpose.

In part, it was political. Her most famous favorite (who was also her longtime lover), Grigory Potemkin, was her right-hand man, top general, and most important political adviser and administrator. Yet the London newspaper that called her "conduct toward her favourites" compelling proof of her "strength of mind" also pointed out that instead of "suffering them to intermeddle in politics (too often the case among favourites here [in Britain] of both sexes in an inferior station) she wisely dismisses them with a handsome allowance, to travel to foreign countries." It seems that, in most cases, favorites were used as her foreign representatives or courtiers rather than given genuine political power. Among some two dozen or more favorites, only Grigory Orlov, Grigory Potemkin, Stanisłaus Poniatowski, Sergei Saltykov, Alexander Yermolov, Pyotr Zavadovsky, and Platon Zubov enjoyed significant political or administrative authority. To be sure, when she needed court allies, they were there to support her, but she did not, for the most part, rely on them in day-to-day political and administrative roles.

If neither primarily romantic nor political, what role, then, did the favorites play? Catherine's biographers point out that, as she aged, the empress anointed younger and younger men as her favorites. In part, this may have been an effort to surround herself with the kind of "joyful" companions she had treasured as a young woman. Perhaps she hoped their youthful vigor would rub off on her. While both of these reasons may have entered into her choice of favorites, it also seems quite apparent that she used the institution of favoritism to educate a rising generation of aristocrats in her own Enlightenment approach to governing. Catherine seems to have been intent on cultivating a new crop of enlightened political and social leaders, but, clearly, she deemed only a select few qualified to rise to positions of genuine leadership. In the end, the creation of a small cadre of well-prepared leaders and administrators may have been the greatest value Catherine secured from the favorites in whom she invested so large a proportion of the imperial treasury.

For the modern business leader, obviously "playing favorites" is not advised. At the very least, an exhibition of favoritism has a demoralizing effect on the organization. In some scenarios, it may even become the basis for legal action on the part of employees who feel unfairly discriminated against. This said, there are elements of Catherine's cultivation of favorites that are worth studying and even emulating. Responsible managers continually identify employees who show promise as future leaders. They cultivate these individuals by providing additional training, mentoring, and even sponsorship for advancement. They give them opportunities to advance, and even a certain amount of room to fail. In this modern game of "playing favorites," the only criteria for inclusion among the favored are promise and performance.

■

Lesson 119
Borrow Best Practices, but Avoid Slavish Imitation

> "This failure proves, as do so many others as well, that in borrowing from others we do not always act in conformity with our own benefit."
>
> ~Catherine, remark in letter to her son Paul concerning the weakness of Russia's military fortifications at Riga, June 1776

Like Peter the Great before her, Catherine the Great was a firm believer in borrowing the best of Western European government, philosophy, medicine, science, and art. For a long time, beginning well before her reign, the Russian army also looked to the West–specifically to Prussia, which was unquestioningly revered as the ideal of modern military practice. As she matured in her reign, however, Catherine began to carefully distinguish between borrowing from Western Europe what a modern business leader would call "best practices" and simply imitating the West indiscriminately.

When Paul, on a tour of the empire at the time, wrote to her about the poor condition of the defenses of the great Baltic Sea port of Riga (today the capital of Latvia), Catherine responded with a warning against the hazards of thoughtless admiration and slavish imitation. The Riga fortifications, she pointed out, had been designed and garrisoned strictly on the Prussian model. Catherine took their inadequate construction as evidence that heedlessly "borrowing from others" was not always to "our own benefit." Russia could only import so much. At some point, it needed to act on its own initiative, with solutions that suited its own specific circumstances.

Business leaders may search for golden nuggets and silver bullets among the examples of how the biggest and most successful corporations "do things." The truth is, however, that business offers no one-size-fits-all solutions. By all means, study your industry. Examine your competitors as closely as possible. Identify best practices *wherever* you find them. Learn from them—even borrow them. But always realize that you must make them your own, modifying and applying every aspect of every process and procedure to suit the goals, resources, market, and personnel of your organization. Slavish imitation is a static attempt to address a dynamic situation. It is bound to fail.

Lesson 120
Use All Circumstances

> "You knew how to use all circumstances in order to elevate the glory of your nation, to conquer your foes, and to compel other nations to seek your friendship and to value it more than any other European nation has ever succeeded in doing."
>
> ~Emperor Joseph II, letter to Catherine II, fall 1780

Along with Frederick II (the Great) of Prussia and Catherine II of Russia, Holy Roman Emperor and Habsburg king Joseph II is deemed one of the three great monarchs of the Enlightenment. Catherine admired him, and, in return, he seems to have admired her even more.

More clearly than anyone but Catherine herself, Joseph understood what she had aimed to accomplish in Russia. Her look toward Western Europe was not merely an act of emulation, but an effort to cultivate–even compel–friendship among the family of the "Enlightened" states. Joseph understood that Catherine approached every circumstance–every diplomatic, economic, cultural, or military interaction with other nations–as an opportunity to "elevate the glory" of Russia, to defeat enemies, and, most important, to position the Russian Empire as a state with which friendship was both desirable and necessary. For example, she offered her services as mediator in the War of the Bavarian Succession (1778–1779), between Austria (on the one side) and Prussia and Saxony (on the other), to gain diplomatic prestige for her empire, and she cultivated a strong but wary alliance with Frederick the Great of Prussia. In his opinion, Catherine had managed this campaign of influence more successfully than "any other European nation," past or present.

Without question, Catherine II was an imperial expansionist. Yet there is a lesson in her program of expansion that reaches well beyond mere conquest for the sake of conquest. She grew her empire strategically in two dimensions. First, she sought physical expansion at the expense of the Ottoman Empire so as to give Russia a Black Sea port. This did for the southern extreme of the empire what Peter the Great's acquisitions and his building of St. Petersburg had done for the North. Both ends of the empire could now communicate and trade with the West.

In conjunction with this strategy of physical expansion, Catherine did all she could to make Russia a presence in Western Europe and a nation with whom the states of the West wanted friendly and productive relations. She sought to enhance the program of Westernization Peter the Great had begun, and while she by no means succeeded in bringing all of Russia into the Age of Enlightenment, she did much to educate her people, to industrialize a significant sector of the economy, and to make her empire a showplace of legal reform. In her alliances with Austria and Prussia, she also demonstrated Russia's value as a military and political ally.

Catherine subordinated everything to these twin strategic goals, using all available circumstances to achieve them. In this there is an important lesson for any strategic leader. Winning for the sake of winning is never a strategically sufficient goal. Any enterprise worth sustaining, let alone growing, must be directed toward genuinely meaningful goals—goals sufficiently compelling to focus every effort on attaining them—so that all tactical circumstances can be directed toward achieving those well-defined, supremely worthwhile ends.

■

Lesson 121
Make a Last Wish

> "My body is to be laid out in a white dress, with a golden crown on the head, on which my forename will be inscribed. Mourning clothes shall be worn half the year, and no longer, the less the better.
>
> "After the first six weeks all the popular amusements should be reopened.
>
> "After the burial, marriages should be permitted–weddings and music."
>
> ~An undated testament in the hand of the empress, quoted in John T. Alexander, *Catherine the Great: Life and Legend*

Catherine left a rich legacy to Russia, including the rudiments (if not the fulfillment) of a rational, transparent, representative government and the skeleton (if not the flesh) of a just body of laws, as well as a vastly expanded empire and one of the greatest art collections in the world. Also revealing, however, is an undated fragmentary testament that she drew up to provide instructions for her funeral and mourning. Consider what the details say about her approach to leadership:

She instructed those responsible for her services to lay her out very simply: white dress and a gold crown bearing nothing more than the name by which her people and the world knew her, "Catherine." She wanted to be remembered adorned only with the essential symbols of her reign, and she wanted to be known by the name to which she had given renown. The memory was to be simple, vivid, precise, and without ambiguity or shading.

She wanted to be mourned–but not for too long. The last thing she desired was to cast a shadow of gloom over her people. Moving forward was more important than stopping to mourn because, in her eyes, the nation was more important than any one leader of it.

She stipulated a return to celebration–"popular amusements" as well as weddings, "with music." The quality she most celebrated in people–especially leaders–was joyfulness.

Whatever the details of the legacy you set out to leave for your organization, take steps to ensure that your memory serves as a source of positive inspiration, satisfaction, and—yes, Catherine's word is appropriate—joy.

■

The Absolute Compromiser

CATHARINE II. ALEXIEVNA. EMPRESS OF RUSSIA. REIGNED XXXV YEARS.

Lesson 122

Master the Art of Compromise

> "What I despair of overthrowing, I undermine."
>
> ~Catherine II to Diderot

Catherine the Great's first notable achievement was surviving her years in the court of Empress Elizabeth, wed to the psychopathic and utterly incompetent Grand Duke Peter. Second to this was her successful overthrow of her husband after he assumed the throne as Czar Peter III.

Not only had Catherine succeeded in fighting her way to power, but she had achieved a throne of absolute authority–at least as defined by history, tradition, and law. Armed with the title and right to unconditional power, it would have been understandable had she, like almost all of her predecessors, commenced a tyrannical reign. For one thing, she was entitled to it. The Russian understanding of "tyrant" was not pejorative or derogatory. It did not imply a monarch of necessarily cruel and oppressive character. Rather, "tyranny" was understood in the classical Greek sense as absolutely authoritarian sovereignty. For another, there was ample historical evidence that the only way to survive on the Russian throne was by inflicting terror. The iconic Russian sovereign, Ivan IV (who ruled from 1547 to 1584), was better known as Ivan the Terrible–a sobriquet that, within Russia, was a description rather than a condemnation. Even the most "enlightened" sovereign prior to Catherine, Peter the Great, fell back on violence and torture when he believed these were necessary. Catherine, however, chose another course, which endured against all odds–at least until the onslaught of the French

Revolution in 1789 prompted her to retreat into a style of governance that more closely resembled the tyranny, if not the terror, of her predecessors.

For most of her reign, Catherine strove to be an enlightened autocrat. She introduced into Russian society an unprecedented degree of representative government, transparency of rule, and administrative competence. Determined to bring her empire into step with the Enlightenment that had swept Western Europe, she opened Russia to virtually all aspects of Western art, science, and political thought. She personally examined and revised the basis of Russian law with the aim of creating a government of laws, not men. To these laws, everyone, from peasant to empress, would be equally subordinate.

Throughout her reign, Catherine remained absolute ruler–"autocratrix"–yet with authority limited by the rational dictates of rational law she herself had imposed by means of her own reformist statement of legal principles, the *Nakaz*. This serious, significant, self-imposed limitation was a decision both intellectual and moral. Catherine was greatly influenced by her reading of Rousseau, Voltaire, and Diderot–reading that was supplemented by correspondence and, in the case of Rousseau and Diderot, conversation. She sincerely believed in a government sufficiently enlightened to do more than compel mass obedience by force. Compelled compliance was unjust and unnatural, she believed. It violated the laws of God as well as human nature. She wanted power, and she wanted authority, but she also wanted to harmonize these with what was just in the minds and hearts of men and within the scheme of Creation.

The self-discipline she imposed on her reign also had a more pragmatic source. She took the common sense view that it was far easier to rule over subjects who approved of you, agreed with you, believed in you, and believed you cared for them than it was to dictate arbitrarily. She subordinated her authority to the laws she herself had largely crafted, and she governed with a sharp eye turned toward public opinion, both within Russia and throughout Europe.

This meant mastering the art of compromise. For example, Catherine was never comfortable with the institution of serfdom, but she believed that summarily abolishing it would bring about rebellion by those who owned serfs. She compromised by retaining serfdom, while also introducing sweeping humanitarian reforms. On August 8, 1762, Catherine issued a decree requiring factory and mine owners who used serf labor to enlist new serf workers at mutually agreeable wages.

It may have seemed to her the ideal compromise, but she soon discovered that the decree produced some unintended consequences. News of the decree prompted currently employed serfs in the Urals and along the Volga to stage massive strikes. Catherine could see no way out of the crisis her well-intentioned decree had triggered other than to break up the strikes with the army. While she gave the commander of the troops, Prince Vyazemsky, authority to use force, she also issued detailed instructions to end the strikes peacefully, telling him to investigate the reasons for the serfs' action and to "do everything you think proper for the satisfaction of the peasants; but [also to] take suitable precautions so that the peasants should not imagine that their managers will be afraid of them in the future. If you find managers guilty of great inhumanity, you may punish them publicly, but if someone has exacted more work than is right, you may punish him secretly; thus you will not give the common people grounds to lose their proper dutifulness."

Her instructions to the prince constituted yet more carefully crafted compromise. Their call for a compromise of outright force was itself subject to compromise, as Catherine cautioned Vyazemsky to avoid doing anything that might make the "peasants . . . imagine that their managers will be afraid of them in the future." She also provided guidelines for punishing misbehaving managers. Those guilty of gross inhumanity were to be publicly punished, whereas those who merely overworked their serfs were to be punished out of view, in secret.

Having ignited unintended consequences with a decree that was perhaps too sweeping, Catherine was determined to create as perfect a compromise between the abolition of serfdom and the enforcement of serfdom as she possibly could, ameliorating the very worst aspects of slavery, yet preserving the institution of servitude on which much of the economic status of the landowning nobility depended. As she explained to Diderot, "What I despair of overthrowing, I undermine."

V. S. Popov, who served as an aide to Grigory Potemkin, related to Alexander I of Russia (1777–1825) a conversation he had had with the young czar's grandmother, Catherine II. Popov recalled that the two conversed about "the unlimited power" with which she "ruled her empire." Popov told the empress that he felt "surprise . . . at the blind obedience with which her will was fulfilled everywhere." Catherine protested: "It is not as easy as you think," she said. "In the first place, my orders would not be carried out unless they were the kind of orders which could be carried out." She explained that she exercised "prudence and circumspection . . . in the promulgation of my laws. I examine the circumstance, I take advice, I consult the enlightened part of the people, and in this way I find out what sort of effect my laws will have." Only when she was "convinced in advance of good approval," did she "issue my orders, and have the pleasure of observing what you call blind obedience." This, she wryly explained, "is the foundation of unlimited power." Then she added: "But, believe me, they will not obey blindly when orders are not adapted to the opinion of the people." Thus, the greatest, most profound, and potentially most wrenching changes–such as abolishing serfdom–had to be enacted gradually, by undermining prejudice and other destructive elements in "the opinion of the people," while introducing positive change incrementally and in harmony with the better part of that opinion. "Unlimited power," even where decreed by history, tradition, and law itself, Catherine knew, was an illusion.

We live in an age of sharply polarized politics, in which a zero-sum, winner-takes-all approach has cast the very idea of compromise into disrepute. The fact is that, in any enterprise with more than a single stakeholder, compromise is both reputable and absolutely necessary. Rare is the situation in which everyone gets everything they want. Your task is not to win at the expense of others in your organization. This is self-defeating. After all, who wants a set of discontented "losers" on the team? Your task, therefore, is to strive for the perfect compromise—an impossible goal in itself. If a compromise were perfect, it would not be a compromise. But in striving toward it, chances are that you will craft the best *feasible* compromise, one that is sufficiently thoughtful to create no unintended consequences and one sufficiently liberal to give as many stakeholders as much of what they want as possible. Reaching this solution may take very considerable time and effort, but no one said leading a business was easy or quick. If the empress of the Russian Empire could accept, embrace, and even invent such limitations on the exercise of her power, so can you. Compromise negotiated from power is a means of both enhancing and sustaining leadership authority by ensuring that it benefits all stakeholders—whether in an empire or an enterprise.

■

A Catherine Chronology

1689–1725

The reign of Peter I, "the Great," inaugurates the historical period of empire in Russia, which will end with the Russian revolution of 1917.

1697–1698

Peter the Great's tour of Europe begins the opening of Russia to the ideas, culture, and politics of the West.

1703

May 27: Peter the Great builds the city St. Petersburg at the mouth of the Neva River on the Gulf of Finland; giving Russia a Baltic port, it serves Peter as what he calls his "window on the West."

1713

The capital of the Russian Empire is officially moved from Moscow to St. Petersburg.

1718

Peter the Great creates a system of "colleges" (*collegia*; singular, *collegium*) to administer major functions of the imperial government; Catherine will extensively reform, rationalize, and modernize these.

1721

October 22: Czar Peter I takes the title "the Great"; he also discards *Czar* in favor of *Emperor,* the Western title by which Russian rulers will be officially known until the end of the monarchy in 1917.

1725

The Russian Academy of Science is founded–an institution Catherine the Great will patronize and expand.

February 8: Peter the Great succumbs to a gangrenous infection of the bladder. According to possibly credible legend, uremia, which periodically plagued him, had been exacerbated by his heroic rescue of a group of soldiers he saw drowning in the semifrozen waters of the Gulf of Finland in November 1724.

1725–1727

Reign of Catherine I, second wife of Peter the Great. She was the first female ruler of Russia, but her humble origins as both a commoner and a servant clouded the succession after her.

1727–1730

Reign of Peter II, grandson of Peter the Great and son of the czarevich, Alexis Petrovich, and Charlotte Christine Sophie, princess of Brunswick-Wolfenbüttel. His succession, based on the forged last will and testament of Catherine I, had sufficient popular support to overcome objections to it. His most significant political act was to bolster the institution of serfdom by forbidding serfs to volunteer for military service–formerly used as an alternative to bondage.

1729

April 21: Sophie Friederike Auguste, princess von Anhalt-Zerbst is born in Stettin to Christian August, prince of Anhalt-Zerbst and a Prussian *Generalfeldmarschall* in the service of Frederick the Great, and Johanna Elisabeth, princess of Holstein-Gottorp.

1730–1740

Reign of Empress Anna, daughter of Ivan V, who had been co-czar of Russia with her uncle, Peter the Great, from 1682 to 1696. Her elevation to the throne was an act of the Russian Supreme Privy Council, who hoped she would be no more than a figurehead. In fact, she proved to be a sadistic tyrant.

1740

May 31: Frederick II (the Great) becomes king of Prussia; with Joseph II of Austria and Catherine, he will be recognized as one of the three great monarchs of the Enlightenment.

October 20: Maria Theresa becomes archduchess of Austria.

1740–1741

October 28 (1740)–December 6 (1741): Reign of Ivan VI, son of Prince Anton Ulrich of Brunswick-Lüneburg and Duchess Anna Leopoldovna of Mecklenburg (niece of Empress Anna and granddaughter of Czar Ivan V). The infant was imprisoned with his family in Dünamünde Fortress after the coup d'état by which Elizabeth seized the throne.

December 6: Peter the Great's daughter, Elizabeth Petrovna, overthrows the infant Czar Ivan VI and becomes Empress Elizabeth of Russia.

December 19: The Danish-Russian explorer Vitus Bering dies (age 60) on what is now Bering Island, Kamchatskaya Oblast, shortly after discovering the Aleutian Islands and mainland Alaska in what was Russia's first contact with the "New World." The strait separating North America from Siberian Russia is named for him.

1741–1762

Reign of Empress Elizabeth, second-oldest surviving daughter of Peter the Great and his second wife, Catherine I.

1744

February: Invited by the Empress Elizabeth I, Sophie arrives in Russia.

June 28: Sophie converts to Russian Orthodoxy, becoming Grand Duchess Catherine.

June 29: Catherine is formally betrothed to Grand Duke Peter, nephew of Elizabeth I.

1745

August 21: Catherine and Peter are wed.

1746

In an effort to limit serfdom, Elizabeth bans the purchase of serfs by commoners.

1752

Catherine begins an affair with Sergei Saltykov, a chamberlain in the court of Elizabeth.

1753

In a move to make the Russian Empire more cohesive, Elizabeth agrees to abolish internal customs and duties between *oblasts* ("districts").

1754

October 1: Catherine's son Pavel Petrovich (Paul I) is born, possibly fathered by Saltykov.

1755

Catherine begins an affair with Stanisław August Poniatowski, whom she will make king of Poland in 1764.

1760

Landowners are given authority to banish unruly serfs to Siberia.

1761–1762

Reign of Peter III, son of Charles Frederick, duke of Holstein-Gottorp, and Anna Petrovna, who was a daughter of Peter the Great and his second wife, Catherine I; Peter III is the nephew of Empress Elizabeth.

1761

Catherine begins an affair with Grigory Orlov, soon to lead the conspiracy to overthrow Peter III.

1762

January 5: Empress Elizabeth I dies, and Catherine's husband ascends the throne as Peter III.

February 18: Peter III issues *Manifesto on the Freedom* [or *Rights*] *of the Nobility,* which freed nobles from compulsory civil and military service (although they were expected to serve in time of war) and allowed nobles to leave and reenter the country at will.

April 11: Catherine gives birth to Aleksei Bobrinsky, fathered by Grigory Orlov.

June 28: Catherine overthrows Peter III and is proclaimed empress of Russia.

July 6: Peter III is (apparently) murdered by Count Aleksey Orlov, a partisan of Catherine the Great.

September 12: Catherine is formally crowned Empress and Autocratrix of All the Russias.

1764

February 26: Catherine decrees the final secularization (seizure) of Orthodox Church lands, thereby ensuring the subordination of the Church to the state.

July 5: Ivan VI, deposed in infancy by Elizabeth in 1741 and held in solitary confinement ever since, was murdered by his jailer to foil an apparent plan to free him. Apparently, when she had seized the throne in 1762, Catherine II had issued a secret standing order to put Ivan VI to death should anyone attempt his release.

November 25: Catherine's former lover, Stanisław Poniatowski, is crowned king of Poland. His presence on the throne, which Catherine engineered against his will, would enable her to bring about three partitions of Poland, by which the kingdom is effectively carved up among Russia, Prussia, and Austria.

1764–1767

As part of her program to ensure settlement of underpopulated regions of the Russian Empire, Catherine the Great encourages the establishment of German immigrant colonies along vast stretches of the lower Volga River.

1765

Catherine sponsors the establishment of the Free Economic Society for the Encouragement of Agriculture and Husbandry, a group dedicated to the study and dissemination of advanced (i.e., Western) methods of farming and estate management.

August 18: On the death of Emperor Francis I, Joseph II becomes emperor of Austria and co-regent with his mother, Maria Theresa. With Catherine and Frederick the Great, Joseph II is regarded as one of the three great monarchs of the Enlightenment.

1766

December: Catherine creates the All-Russia Legislative Commission to implement the legal code outlined in her treatise, *The Great Instruction* (*Nakaz*).

1768–1774

First Russo-Turkish War

1769

May: Grigory Potemkin volunteers to Catherine for service in the first Russo-Turkish War.

1770

July 5–7: The Russian navy wins a spectacular victory at the Battle of Chesma, virtually annihilating the Ottoman fleet.

July 7: Potemkin is decorated for his conspicuous gallantry.

1771

February 12: Gustav III becomes king of Sweden after leading a coup d'état.

1772

August 5: The First Partition of Poland is instituted.

1773

Catherine replaces Grigory Orlov with a new court favorite and lover, Alexander Vasilchikov, a young officer who also serves as her valet.

1773–1775

The Pugachev Rebellion poses a serious challenge to Catherine's ability to administer her empire. It begins as a rebellion of Yaik Cossacks led by Yemelyan Pugachev, a former imperial army officer. Claiming to be Peter III–he tells a tale of his narrow escape in 1762 from Catherine's usurping clutches–Pugachev briefly creates a rival Russian government and, among other things, proclaims the abolition of serfdom.

1774

January: Potemkin returns to St. Petersburg and replaces Vasilchikov as Catherine's favorite and lover; some historians believe he and Catherine are secretly married.

May 10: Louis XVI is crowned king of France; Marie Antoinette is his queen.

July 21: The Treaty of Kücük Kaynarca ends the Russo-Turkish War and proclaims the Crimea independent of the Ottoman Empire, effectively delivering the region to the Russian Empire; thus, as Peter the Great had expanded the Russian Empire westward in the north, Catherine has now expanded it westward
in the south.

1775

January 21: The rebel Yemelyan Pugachev is publicly executed, drawn, and quartered in Moscow.

1776

Potemkin is replaced as Catherine's lover and favorite by Pyotr Zavadovsky, her secretary; he nevertheless remains a close and key adviser to the empress.

July 4: The American colonies declare their independence from the British Crown.

1777

Semyon Zorich, a military officer, replaces Zavadovsky as Catherine's favorite and lover.

December 23: Aleksandr Pavlovich (later Emperor Alexander I) is born to Catherine's son, Grand Duke Pavel Petrovich (later Emperor Paul I).

1780

Alexander Lanskoy, aide-de-camp to Grigory Potemkin, replaces Zorich as Catherine's favorite and lover.

November 29: Maria Theresa dies, leaving Joseph II as sole ruling emperor of Austria.

1781

Joseph II and Catherine conclude an alliance between their respective countries, Austria and Russia.

1781–1786

During this period, the Ukraine is fully absorbed into the Russian Empire–a further grand imperial expansion under Catherine the Great.

1783

For the first time in Russian history, private ownership and operation of printing presses is authorized.

1783–1786

Grigory Shelikhov (1747–1795), seafarer and merchant, founds the first permanent Russian settlements in North America in what is now coastal Alaska; these became bases for the Russian fur trade on the continent.

1783–1787

The Italian architect Giacomo Quarenghi (1744–1817) builds the Hermitage Theater, the most spectacular of the enlargements and elaborations of St. Petersburg's Winter Palace (familiarly called the Hermitage) commissioned by Catherine the Great. Catherine housed her great and growing collection of Western European art in the Winter Palace. Her acquisitions would be the basis for the vast collection of what would become in 1852 the Imperial Hermitage Museum and that is now the State Hermitage Museum, a display of artworks second in size only to the Louvre in Paris.

1784

February: Acting on Catherine's orders, Potemkin founds the Black Sea port city of Sevastopol.

February 2: Catherine creates the Taurida Governorate to administer the newly annexed Crimea.

1785

April 21: Catherine promulgates *Charter for the Rights, Freedoms, and Privileges of the Noble Russian Gentry* (*Charter to the Gentry*), which recognizes the "corps of nobles" in each Russian province as a legal corporate body with considerable autonomy. As a class, the gentry is now exempted from taxation and judicial corporal punishment, is given total control of revenue and other economic gains generated by their serfs, is given the irrevocable right of assembly, and is granted the privilege of trial in courts constituted of and by their own kind.

1786

Alexander Dmitriev-Mamonov, another Potemkin aide-de-camp, becomes Catherine's new favorite and lover.

August 17: Frederick the Great of Prussia dies; Frederick William II succeeds him.

1787–1791

The Second Russo-Turkish War is fought; Joseph II reluctantly brings Austria into the war as a Russian ally (1788).

1788–1790

After Gustav III attacks Russia, the Russo-Swedish War is fought.

1789

The courtier Platon Zubov replaces Dmitriev-Mamonov as Catherine's favorite and, possibly, lover.

1789

July 14: The French Revolution begins with the storming of the Bastille. The outbreak and course of the revolution, particularly the execution of Louis XVI and Marie Antoinette, prompt Catherine to eschew most of the Enlightenment ideology that has hitherto guided her reign.

1790

Aleksandr Radishchev publishes *A Journey from St. Petersburg to Moscow*, which is highly critical of Catherine's Russia—especially with regard to serfdom and the unchecked power of the nobility. Catherine condemns the book as radical and orders it banned and burned. Initially sentenced to death, Radishchev wins from Catherine commutation to Siberian exile and is freed by her son and successor, Paul I.

February 20: Emperor Joseph II dies, apparently of an illness contracted in 1788 during his participation in Catherine's second war against the Ottoman Empire.

July 9–10: In the Second Battle of Svensksund, a Swedish fleet under Gustav III delivers a ruinous defeat against the Russian fleet commanded by Prince Charles of Nassau-Siegen; 7,400 Russians are killed, wounded, or captured, fifty-one Russian ships are lost, and twenty-two more taken as prizes.

August 14: Despite his overwhelming naval victory in July, Gustav III signs the Treaty of Värälä with Catherine, restoring the status quo antebellum, neither side gaining anything.

1791

October 16: Potemkin dies of a fever contracted while negotiating at Catherine's behest the Treaty of Jassy, which would end the Second Russo-Turkish War early the following year.

1792

January 9: The Treaty of Jassy ends the Second Russo-Turkish War by confirming Russian dominance on the Black Sea.

March 29: Gustav III of Sweden is assassinated.

1793

January 23: The Second Partition of Poland is implemented.

September 2: The Russian Senate seeks to proclaim Catherine "MOTHER of the Fatherland" and "dedicate to [her] forename the sobriquet GREAT." She humbly declines the titles–though history will nevertheless remember her as "Catherine the Great."

1794

March 24: Tadeusz Kościuszko, Polish hero of the American Revolution, begins an uprising against Russian rule in Poland; the uprising is crushed by November 16.

1795

October 24: The Third Partition of Poland is implemented.

1796

July 6: Nikolay Pavlovich (later Emperor Nicholas I), Catherine's third grandson, is born.

November 17: Catherine the Great dies of an apparent stroke; Paul I ascends the throne.

1796–1801

Reign of Paul I, Catherine the Great's son.

1801

March 23: Outraged by Paul I's efforts to revive the liberal Enlightenment reform agenda his mother had largely abandoned, a cabal of noblemen and military officers conspires to assassinate him; he is brutally murdered in his own bedroom.

1801–1825

Reign of Alexander I, Catherine the Great's grandson.

Dramatis Personae

Alexander I (1777–1825)

Son of Czar Paul I and grandson of Catherine II, Aleksandr Pavlovich assumed the Russian throne on the assassination of his father on March 24, 1801 (he was formally crowned on September 15). He also reigned as the first Russian king of Poland (from 1815 to 1825) and as the first Russian grand duke of Finland and Lithuania.

The first of four brothers, he was born near the end of Catherine's reign. The empress took personal charge of raising him and his brother Constantine, and some authorities believe that she planned to engineer Aleksandr's succession to the throne in place of his father, her son Paul, who had fallen out of favor with her.

Aleksandr imbibed much of the Enlightenment progressivism of Catherine's court prior to the era of the French Revolution. Both his grandmother and his own Swiss tutor, Frédéric-César de La Harpe, introduced him to Rousseau's theories of "natural man." At the same time, Catherine exposed her grandson to the instruction of Field Marshal Nikolay Saltykov, who served as his "permanent military tutor." (Saltykov was a member of the noble family that also produced Sergei Saltykov, Catherine's first favorite and first documented lover.) The field marshal had little patience with the likes of Rousseau and indoctrinated the boy into the ways of a militaristic Russian autocracy.

Catherine also played a key role in matching Aleksandr with Louise of Baden, whom he married in 1793, when he was but fifteen and she fourteen. Three years later, Catherine died, removing any doubt that his father, not he, would succeed the empress. When Czar Paul I was murdered by a group of dismissed Russian army officers on March 23, 1801, Aleksandr became Emperor Alexander I. He embarked on a program of domestic reform driven by the same Enlightenment ideals that had inspired his grandmother. His radical objective, at least initially, was to effect evolutionary change toward a constitutional monarchy and the abolition of serfdom. He fell short of this goal but did repeal the long-standing prohibition against ownership of land by commoners.

Alexander I's greatest challenge came from Napoléon, against whom he championed a coalition of European nations and rallied Russia to a "holy war" against Napoléon. Defeated at the Battle of Friedland (June 14, 1807), however, Alexander I executed an abrupt about-face, summarily accepting Napoléon's offer to join him in a world-dominating alliance. It did not last long, and in 1812 Napoléon invaded Russia and burned Moscow before beginning a long and ultimately ruinous winter retreat.

The final defeat of Napoléon at Waterloo in 1815 left Alexander I, who had become profoundly religious after the ordeal of the invasion, the most powerful monarch in Europe. His former Enlightenment liberalism turned reactionary, and he himself became paranoid, increasingly suspicious of internal plots against him. His health declined rapidly, and he succumbed to typhus on December 1, 1825.

Augustus III of Poland (1696–1763)

Augustus III reigned as king of Poland from October 17, 1696, until his death on October 5, 1763. He had come to the throne as a result of a war of succession against followers of Stanisław Leszczyński (Stanisław I), in which his own claim to power was supported by Peter the Great of Russia. Eager to place on the throne a ruler who would not resist Russian domination of Poland, Catherine II blocked Augustus III's later attempt to position his family for succession. She engineered the ascension of her former favorite and lover Stanisław August Poniatowski upon the death of Augustus III.

Betskoy, Ivan (1704–1795)

Ivan Betskoy began his career as aide-de-camp to his field marshal father. After further service as a diplomat, he was instrumental in the coup d'état that brought Peter the Great's daughter, Yelizaveta Petrovna, to the Russian throne as Elizabeth I. When Peter III ascended the Russian throne following Elizabeth's death in 1762, he appointed Betskoy supervisor of the imperial palaces and gardens. Almost immediately, Betskoy began to conspire with Catherine and others to overthrow Peter III.

Upon her ascension to the throne, Catherine named Betskoy to the presidency of the Imperial Academy of Arts in 1764. In addition to serving as her cultural adviser and encouraging her interest in the Enlightenment philosophers he had known in Paris, Betskoy worked closely with Catherine to reform Russian schools based on Enlightenment precepts and to create the empire's first system of public education. He collaborated with the empress in writing the treatise *On the Duties of Man and Citizen.* Along with his work in educational reform, Betskoy championed the establishment of state-sponsored foundling homes in Moscow (1764) and St. Petersburg (1770).

Bibikov, Aleksandr (1729–1774)

A career military officer, Bibikov fought in the Seven Years' War (1756–1763), emerging from the conflict with the rank of colonel. He fought to suppress insurrection in Poland from 1771 to 1773. Immediately after this, Catherine ordered him to lead units in the suppression of Pugachev's Rebellion. In 1774, during this campaign, he contracted cholera, to which he succumbed.

Bielke, Frau Johanna Dorothea (fl. 1770s)

Little is known of this woman, except that she conducted a rich correspondence with Catherine II from 1772 to 1774 and clearly enjoyed the confidence and affection of the empress, who wrote to her in a particularly frank and open manner.

Bobrinsky (Bobrinskoy), Aleksie (1762–1813)

Born on April 11, 1762, before Catherine assumed the throne, he was her natural son by her favorite and lover, Count Grigory Orlov. Named for Aleksey Orlov, his uncle and godfather, the infant was raised in the village of Bobriki, from which his surname, Bobrinsky, was derived. Paul I, who succeeded his mother, Catherine, on her death in 1796, publicly acknowledged him as his half-brother and, on day five of his reign, elevated him to count and conferred on him the military rank of general-major. Married to Baroness Anna Dorothea von Ungern-Sternberg, he fathered a noble line that survives to this day.

Brümmer, Otto (fl. 1730s–60s)

Officially grand marshal of the court of Grand Duke Peter (later, Catherine's husband and Czar Peter III), Brümmer supervised the upbringing of the eleven-year-old grand duke after the death of his father in 1739. The aloof brutality with which he abused young Peter may well have contributed to the creation of that hapless individual's own apparently twisted nature.

Catherine I (1684–1727)

The second wife of Peter I (the Great), the mother of Elizabeth I, and the namesake of Catherine II, Catherine I succeeded Peter I, reigning from February 8, 1725 until her death on May 17, 1727, as the first female ruler of the Russian Empire.

She had been born, in Latvia, Marta Elena Skarrońska, probably the daughter of a Lithuanian peasant of Polish origin. Her parents died in an epidemic of plague when she was three years old, whereupon an aunt took her to live in Marienburg, near the Latvian border with Estonia and Russia. Here she was entrusted to the care of a Lutheran pastor, Johann Ernst Glück, who "employed" her as his housemaid. At seventeen, Marta was married briefly to a Swedish dragoon, eventually becoming a servant in the household of Prince Alexander Menshikov, after the Russians captured Marienburg. While visiting Menshikov, Peter I became enamored of Marta and made her his mistress. She converted to Orthodoxy in 1705 and took the name of Yekaterina Alekseyevna. Two years later, she and the czar secretly married. They were not publicly married until 1712. The couple had a dozen children, only two of whom, including the future Empress Elizabeth, survived to adulthood.

In 1724 Catherine I was officially named co-ruler, and when Peter died on February 8, 1725, without having named a successor, Catherine I, supported by the army, was named empress.

Choglokov, Nicholas (fl. mid-eighteenth century)

A court chamberlain employed by Elizabeth I as a governor for Grand Duke Peter, Choglokov was described by Catherine the Great as "an arrogant, brutal fool; a stupid, conceited, malicious, pompous, secretive and silent man who never smiled; a man to be despised as well as feared." His wife was Maria Semenovna Choglokova, who served as Elizabeth's "watchdog" over Catherine.

Choglokova, Maria Semenovna (fl. mid-eighteenth century)
The wife of Nicholas Choglokov, Grand Duke Peter's disagreeable governor, Madame Choglokova was the Empress Elizabeth's first cousin. She served as Elizabeth's "watchdog," reporting to Elizabeth Catherine's every word and act.

Christian August, Prince of Anhalt-Zerbst (1690–1747)
Catherine the Great's father, Christian August, was prince of Anhalt-Zerbst and, in the service of Frederick the Great, a Prussian *Generalfeldmarschall.* His early career was in the military, beginning in 1708 with service in the regiment guard and, in 1709, with membership in the 8th Regiment of Foot (later called the Grenadier's Regiment King Frederick William IV of Prussia). By 1741, he was an infantry general, who also served as governor of Stettin. In May of the following year, Frederick the Great elevated him to *Generalfeldmarschall*, the highest rank in the Prussian service. That same year, the death of his cousin John Augustus, Prince of Anhalt-Zerbst, made him and his brother, John Louis II, co-rulers of the principality. When John Louis II died in 1746, Christian August became sole ruler of the principality–until his own death just four months later.

Christian August had married Johanna Elisabeth of Holstein-Gottorp on November 8, 1727. It was not a particularly happy marriage, since she was considerably younger than he and had come from a far more powerful and distinguished family, which was in the line of the Swedish succession. Nevertheless, the union produced five children, including Sophie Friederike Auguste, who would become Catherine II (the Great).

Diderot, Denis (1713–1784)
A prominent intellectual and artistic figure of the French Enlightenment, Diderot was not only among Catherine's numerous intellectual correspondents, he was also her guest for several months in St. Petersburg. Despite his literary and cultural

renown, Diderot was chronically short of cash. Catherine came to his rescue by purchasing his extensive library for a generous price. She then asked that he keep the volumes in Paris until she should ask for them. In the meantime, she employed him as her librarian at a substantial salary, thereby effectively subsidizing him in his later years. Catherine also hired Diderot to select artworks for her collection, which became the core of what is today the Hermitage State Museum of Art, one of the world's biggest and oldest art museums.

Diderot is best known as the cofounder, editor, and major contributor to the *Encyclopédie,* an intellectual endeavor of boundless ambition, intended to "change men's common way of thinking."

Dimsdale, Dr. Thomas (1712–1800)

A native of Essex, England, Dimsdale served in 1745 as a surgeon with the Duke of Cumberland's army during the suppression of the Jacobite Rising to restore the Stuart dynasty in Great Britain. A passionate advocate of smallpox inoculation, he wrote an important early treatise on the subject, *The Present Method of Inoculating for the Small-Pox*, in 1767. Among those who read the work was Catherine II, who summoned Dimsdale to St. Petersburg in 1768 to inoculate her and her son and heir, Grand Duke Paul. She successfully set an example that was emulated throughout her court and, ultimately, throughout her empire.

Dimsdale went on to write more works on inoculation and was a founder of the financial firm that would become the Royal Bank of Scotland.

Dmitriev-Mamonov, Alexander (1758–1803)

Descended from princes of Smolensk, Dimitriev-Mamonov was appointed aide-de-camp to Grigory Potemkin in 1784. In 1786, Potemkin introduced him to Catherine II, who made him a favorite and a lover. She elevated him to the office of chamberlain in the

St. Petersburg court and assigned him lavish apartments in the Winter Palace.

Dimitriev-Mamonov soon tired of his relationship with the sixty-year-old empress and began an affair with her sixteen-year-old lady-in-waiting, the Princess Shcherbatova. When the affair resulted in his marriage to the princess, Catherine presented the couple with an extraordinary wedding present of 100,000 rubles and 2,500 serfs–along with an order of banishment from St. Petersburg.

Elizabeth I (1709–1762)

Elizabeth–Yelizaveta Petrovna–was born to Peter the Great and Catherine I two years after they were secretly married. The fact that the marriage had not been public at the time of her birth prompted many to challenge Elizabeth's right to succeed to the throne, especially given her mother's humble origin as a common servant. While Peter lavished affection on her, he did not groom her to succeed him.

After Peter the Great's death in 1725, Catherine I ascended the throne, with Prince Alexander Menshikov in effect ruling as the power behind the throne. When she died two years later, Peter the Great's grandson, Pyotr Alekseyevich became emperor as Peter II. Menshikov attempted to prolong what amounted to his own regency, but was overthrown by Prince Ivan Dolgorukov and exiled to Siberia. Elizabeth was also effectively banished.

Early in 1730, Peter II died and was succeeded by the Empress Anna, a niece of Peter the Great. Elizabeth quietly conspired to gather support for her own ascension to the throne. When Anna died in 1730, the infant Ivan VI became emperor under the incompetent regency of Grand Duchess Anna Leopoldovna. General corruption of government and economic crisis created an opportunity for Elizabeth to seize power in a bloodless coup carried out with the help of the elite Preobrazhensky Regiment, which had been fiercely loyal to its founder, her father.

The coup was the last truly vigorous act of government the Empress Elizabeth performed. Her principal preoccupation was to establish an unchallenged line of succession, and it was for this that she arranged a marriage between her nephew, the grand duke Peter (Karl Peter Ulrich) of Holstein-Gottorp and Sophie of Anhalt-Zerbst, the future Catherine II. Elizabeth's reign ended with her death on January 5, 1762, apparently of a stroke.

Falconet, Étienne-Maurice (1716–1791)

Upon the recommendation of Denis Diderot, Catherine the Great invited this Paris-born sculptor–at the time, director of the sculpture studio of the royal porcelain works at Sévre–to design and execute a monumental statue of Peter the Great in St. Petersburg. Falconet arrived in Russia in 1766, but it was 1775 before casting of the statue began, by which time Falconet had returned to France (see Lesson 30, "Make Your Point Monumental").

Frederick II (the Great) of Prussia (1712–1786)

Frederick II, known as Frederick the Great, defined Enlightenment absolutism (called by some "enlightened despotism") during his reign as a king *in* Prussia (1740–1772) and as king *of* Prussia (1772–1786). He was a sometime ally and sometime foe of Catherine II, but also invariably served her as a model of Enlightenment rule. With Catherine the Great and Joseph II of Austria, Frederick the Great is considered one of the trio of outstanding Enlightenment monarchs. He laid the foundation of the modern empire and state of Germany, drawing together disparate and fractious principalities around the nucleus of Prussia. In so doing, he profoundly transformed European politics and history.

Frederick was born in Berlin on January 24, 1712, the son of the Prussian king Frederick William I and Sophia Dorothea of Hanover, the daughter of England's King George I. When his father died on May 21, 1740, Frederick inherited the crown, an event that prompted sneers from observers all across Europe. They believed Frederick would make a weak show after the sternly authoritative rule of his father. Frederick's many critics were proved wrong. In the course of his career, he would not only show himself to be an able military commander and, at times, a brilliant strategist, but also the model of the "enlightened despot."

When Russia, France, and Austria became allies in 1756, Frederick invaded Saxony and started the Seven Years' War. The death of Empress Elizabeth of Russia took that country out of the war and thereby allowed Frederick to make peace with the other powers. On the surface, this long and costly war had resulted in no positive gains for any of the belligerents. Yet Frederick had succeeded in demonstrating to the world that he was a military genius and that Prussia was a power to be reckoned with. In 1772, Frederick was instrumental in the First Partition of Poland among Catherine's Russia, Joseph's Austria, and his own Prussia.

In August 1786, Frederick reviewed his troops in Potsdam during a downpour. Drenched, he caught a chill, sickened, and died several days later on August 17.

Geoffrin, Madame Marie Thérèse Rodet (1699–1777)

The daughter of Pierre Rodet, a *valet de chambre* for the duchess of Burgundy, and Angelique Thérèse Chemineau, a banker's daughter, Marie Thérèse Rodet, at thirteen, was married to François Geoffrin, a wealthy forty-nine-year-old widower. As a result, she was later able to finance weekly "*salons*," extraordinary gatherings in her Parisian house to which the luminaries of the French Enlightenment were invited for conversation. By the time she was thirty, Madame Geoffrin was the most celebrated hostess in Paris, and her *salons* became the talk of Europe. Moreover, the example she set inspired many others. She established the pattern for one of the great cultural institutions of the Enlightenment.

Among her many prominent correspondents throughout Europe was Empress Catherine II, whose letters to Madame Geoffrin are often intimate and revelatory, as well as brilliant.

Grimm, Friedrich Melchior, Baron (1723–1807)

Born, raised, and educated in Germany—a student at the University of Leipzig—Grimm, in 1748, accompanied August Heinrich, Count Friesen, to Paris as his secretary. In this city, he was befriended by none other than Jean-Jacques Rousseau, through whom he became associated with the other leading figures of the French Enlightenment.

In 1753, Grimm began publishing for private subscription among a circle of German sovereigns a cultural and intellectual newsletter he called *Correspondance littéraire, philosophique et critique*. Before long, circulation of the newsletter spread beyond the original circle, reaching both Catherine the Great and Stanisław Poniatowski, the young man she had placed on the Polish throne. Catherine met Grimm personally in 1773, when he was in St. Petersburg to attend the marriage of Wilhelmina Louisa of Hesse-Darmstadt to her son Paul. Although he became the ambassador of Saxe-Gotha to France in 1776, he managed to return to St. Petersburg in 1777 and was hosted by Catherine for almost a year. She relished his conversation and cultural insights, and she commissioned him as her agent to acquire artworks in Paris for the Hermitage collection. Catherine thought so highly of Grimm that, when he fell on hard times in 1796, she appointed him minister of Russia at Hamburg, a sinecure that assured him financial security for the rest of his life.

Gustav III of Sweden (1746–1792)

Gustav III seized the Swedish throne by a coup d'état in 1772, hoping thereby to restore the absolute autocracy that had been diluted by parliamentarianism during Sweden's so-called Age of Liberty, which followed the death of Charles XII. Like Catherine in Russia, Gustav sought to rule as an *enlightened* absolutist. He ran afoul of Catherine, however, when he sought her support in wresting Norway from Danish possession. The empress refused to betray her ally, Denmark, and so Gustav responded by declaring war on Russia.

The Russo-Swedish War spanned 1788–1790 and was mostly inconclusive until Gustav managed to inflict a catastrophic naval defeat against the Russian fleet at the Battle of Svensksund on July 9, 1790. This prompted Catherine to make peace the next month and, in 1791, even to conclude with Sweden a defensive alliance.

Gustav fell victim to a conspiracy of reactionary aristocrats, one of whom shot him in the back on March 16, 1792. He died thirteen days later.

Gyllenborg, Count Henning (1713–1775)

The nephew of Swedish foreign minister Carl Gyllenborg, Henning Gyllenborg encountered a teenaged Sophie (the future Catherine II) first in Hamburg and, later, in St. Petersburg. He guided her early reading in history and philosophy and counseled her mother, Johanna, to respect the girl's formidable intellect.

Ivan VI (1740–1764)

The son of Prince Anton Ulrich of Brunswick-Lüneburg and Duchess Anna Leopoldovna of Mecklenburg, niece of Empress Anna of Russia and granddaughter of Czar Ivan V, Ivan Antonovich was adopted by Anna, who declared him her successor. He was duly proclaimed Emperor Ivan VI on October 29, 1740, the day after Anna's death. Just thirteen months later, however, Elizabeth I seized the throne through a coup d'état, and the infant emperor and his family were confined to Riga before being locked away, on December 13, 1742, in the fortress of Dünamünde. Two years after this, Ivan was separated from his family and imprisoned at Kholmogory on the White Sea.

When Peter III succeeded his aunt in 1762, it looked as if Ivan might be at long last liberated, but Catherine's overthrow of her erstwhile husband just six months after he assumed the throne ended this prospect. When a junior officer of the garrison at the Shlisselburg fortress, where Ivan was now housed, led an attempt to free him, the young man's jailers murdered their prisoner to prevent his release.

Johanna Elisabeth, Princess of Holstein-Gottorp (1712–1760)

A princess raised in the court of Brunswick, Johanna was married to a provincial princeling and general in the Prussian army, Christian August of Anhalt-Zerbst. Their daughter, Sophie, was invited to the court of Elizabeth of Russia to become the bride of Grand Duke Peter, heir to the Russian throne. Johanna accompanied her daughter to St. Petersburg, and Sophie married Peter, thereby becoming Grand Duchess Catherine–and, unforeseen at the time, the future empress Catherine II (Catherine the Great). Having managed to alienate the Empress Elizabeth, however, Johanna was sent packing back to Anhalt-Zerbst shortly after the wedding. Widowed in 1747, she ruled the principality as regent to her son until 1752, when she retired to Paris to live out the rest of her life.

Joseph II (1741–1790)

With Catherine the Great and Frederick the Great, Joseph II, Holy Roman Emperor and ruler of the Habsburg lands, completes the historic trio of the great Enlightenment monarchs.

Joseph was the eldest son of Maria Theresa and her husband, Francis I. He was also the brother of Marie Antoinette. Like both Catherine and Frederick, he was an exemplar of enlightened absolutism, which some call, more pejoratively, "enlightened despotism." He made ambitious efforts to introduce reforms in the law, in education, and in medicine, and he sought to make the administration of government generally more efficient. In all of this, he achieved only a limited degree of success, Austria being an inherently conservative realm in the eighteenth century.

As the somewhat reluctant ally of Catherine the Great, he fought the Austro-Turkish War of 1787–1791 concurrently with Catherine's Russo-Turkish War of 1787–1792—though with considerably fewer gains to show for it than was the case for Russia. Indeed, Joseph's personal leadership at the front caused him to fall ill with one of the fevers endemic to the region, and he died shortly after returning to Vienna.

Montesquieu, Charles-Louis de Secondat, Baron de Le Bréde et de (1689–1755)

One of the most important social thinkers of the French Enlightenment, Montesquieu was the author of *De l'Esprit des Lois* (*The Spirit of the Laws*), published in 1748 and arguing in favor of constitutional government, the principle of separation of powers, the preservation of civil liberties, and an end to slavery. Catherine the Great borrowed extensively from this work in creating *The Great Instruction* (*Nakaz*), her ambitious attempt to revise and rationalize the chaotic body of Russian law.

Orlov, Grigory (1734–1783)

One of four politically important Orlov brothers, Grigory fought in the Seven Years' War (1756–1763). While serving in St. Petersburg during that war, he made a deep impression on Grand Duchess Catherine (she was not yet empress). The two became lovers, and Orlov assumed leadership of the cabal that overthrew her erstwhile husband, Peter III.

Having ascended the throne, Catherine made Orlov a count and promoted him to adjutant-general, director-general of engineers, and general-in-chief. Shortly after she became empress, their illegitimate son, Alexie, was born.

Orlov served Catherine faithfully as a counselor during the early years of her reign and was among her court favorites. He was instrumental in the creation of the All-Russia Legislative Commission of 1767, which was tasked with implementing the principles of Catherine's *Great Instruction* (*Nakaz*). He failed, however, in the diplomatic role Catherine assigned him in 1771, to craft a lasting peace with the Ottoman Empire, and he was soon replaced as Catherine's favorite (and lover) by Grigory Potemkin.

Panin, Nikita (1718–1783)

Panin served as Catherine the Great's adviser and political mentor for the first eighteen years of her reign. His dream of a Northern Alliance–never fully realized–would have bound together Russia, Prussia, Poland, and Sweden against France and Austria. Panin also promoted closer ties with Prussia. His influence in Catherine's court ultimately declined, however, because of his persistent jealousy over her many lovers (which did not include him) and because of his opposition to the partition of Poland.

Paul I (1754–1801)

Catherine's son–officially by her husband, Grand Duke Peter (Peter III), but possibly by her lover at the time, Sergei Saltykov–Pavel Petrovich was raised mainly by the Empress Elizabeth and was tutored intensively by the man who would serve as Catherine's own mentor, Nikita Panin. After Paul's first wife died in childbirth (along with the child), Catherine, eager for heirs, efficiently brokered a marriage with Sophia Dorothea of Württemberg, who converted to the Orthodox faith as Maria Fyodorovna. Catherine may even have been planning to exclude Paul from the line of succession, in order to advance his elder son, Aleksandr Pavlovich, to the throne; however, she died without having taken action to make this happen. Paul therefore succeeded his mother on November 17, 1796.

His attempts to revive the spirit of the Enlightenment, which his mother had abandoned after the onset of the French Revolution, alienated conservative elements in his court, and, on

March 23, 1801, he was assassinated–stabbed and trampled to death in his own bedroom.

Peter I the Great (1672–1725)

Born on June 6, 1672, in Moscow, to Czar Feodor III Alakseevich and his second wife, Natalia Kirillovna Naryshkina, Peter himself was proclaimed czar when he was only ten years old, in 1682, upon the death of his father. Later that year, however, the *streltsi*–"militia musketeers"–staged a revolt, forcing the boy to share the throne with his "imbecile" brother Ivan V under the regency of their sister Sophia. During this early period, young Peter became interested in the world beyond Russia and developed a passion for European culture, learning, fashion, and military practices. Living outside Moscow in Preobrazhenskoye, he formed two elite regiments of guards and plotted with his guardian, Prince Boris Golitsyn, the overthrow of Sophia. Golitsyn moved successfully against Sophia in August 1689, and Peter took control of the government.

Peter undertook military expeditions to the White Sea during 1694–1695 and wrested the Azov region from Turkish control during 1695–1696. Following this conquest, he realized an ambition nurtured since childhood–to travel to Europe. From March 1697 to August 1698, he toured Germany, Britain, and the Netherlands, hungrily observing examples of the most advanced technology and science then available as well as examples of Western European fashion, style, and mores. Peter was forced to cut short his tour when news reached him of another *streltsi* revolt, which he put down with savage fury during the course of the summer of 1698.

After crushing the *streltsi*, Peter set about a program of commensurately vigorous social reform and also remodeled his army. Introducing conscription, he drafted some 32,000 commoners, allied himself with Augustus II of Poland and Saxony in November 1699, and attacked the Swedes in Livonia in

August 1700. Peter's military ambition outstripped his skill as a commander, and he was defeated by Swedish king Charles XII at the Battle of Narva on November 30, 1700.

The young monarch did not give up, however, and continued efforts to transform Russia into a European-style industrial and military power. Peter established factories, arms manufacturers, and military schools. He developed a system of internal transport, as well as encouraged the growth of a shipbuilding industry in order to open up commerce with the rest of the world. Having learned from his defeat at Narva to put his trust in good military advisers, he secured the leadership of Field Marshal Count Sheremetev in an invasion of Ingria, then held by the Swedes. On January 9, 1702, Peter and Sheremetev defeated a Swedish army at Erestfer and then, on July 29, at Hummelshof in Livonia. Peter occupied the valley of the Neva River in December 1702, and he founded the city of St. Petersburg on May 16, 1703, as his "window on the West."

From June 12 to August 21, 1704, Peter besieged Narva, this time successfully. His ally, Augustus II, had surrendered to Charles XII of Sweden when Peter, now holding Narva, proposed a peace with the Swedish monarch. Charles angrily rejected the offer and invaded Russia during 1707–1708, but was decisively defeated on July 8, 1709 at the Battle of Poltava.

Having disposed of the northern threat for the time being, Peter turned next to the south, moving against Turkish Moldavia in March of 1711. Outmaneuvered by Turkish forces, he was hemmed in at the River Pruth and was compelled to negotiate a settlement on July 21, 1711. Three years later, Peter again directed his efforts against the Swedes, planning with Admiral Feodor Apraskin a devastating attack on the Swedish fleet near Hangö in the Baltic on July 7, 1714. By this single, masterful stroke, Peter gained control of the Baltic Sea, including the prizes of Livonia, Estonia, Ingria, and southern Karelia, which were ceded to Russia by treaty on August 30, 1721.

With his empire greatly expanded, his court Europeanized, and the fractious nobility more unified than they had ever before been, Peter I exchanged the Russian title of *czar* for the Western title of *emperor* on November 2, 1721. He died on February 8, 1725, in his beloved St. Petersburg from complications of a cold he had caught while helping to rescue soldiers who had fallen into the frozen Neva River.

Peter III (1728–1762)

Karl Peter Ulrich was born, in Kiel, to Charles Frederick, duke of Holstein-Gottorp, and Anna Petrovna, a daughter of Peter the Great and Catherine I. Anna Petrovna died just three months after Peter's birth, and his father died in 1739, leaving the eleven-year-old an orphan with the title of duke of Holstein-Gottorp. He was adopted by Empress Elizabeth of Russia, who brought him to St. Petersburg in 1742 and proclaimed him heir presumptive to the imperial throne.

Peter had no affection for Russia or the Russians, and he had no strong desire to become the country's ruler. Nevertheless, Elizabeth brokered a marriage with his second cousin, Sophie Friederike Auguste, the daughter of Christian August, prince of Anhalt-Zerbst, and Johanna Elisabeth of Holstein-Gottorp. After her conversion to the Orthodox faith, she was renamed Catherine, after Elizabeth's mother.

Popular culture portrays Peter as deranged, depraved, and developmentally disabled. This picture is probably exaggerated, but there can be little doubt that he was in many ways infantile (he played with dolls and toy soldiers), that he was inherently cruel (he delighted in torturing animals), that he became an alcoholic, that he showed only contempt for Catherine, that he was unfaithful to her (as she was to him), and that he was probably little interested in conducting affairs of state. Peter and Catherine were married on August 21, 1745, and produced a son, Pavel (who would reign as Paul I), and a daughter, Anna Petrovna, who lived only two years. Many historians believe that Paul was actually fathered by

Sergei Saltykov, an early lover and favorite of Catherine. Others, however, point to a family resemblance between Paul and Peter, suggesting that he was, in fact, the boy's father.

Peter ascended the throne on January 5, 1762, upon the death of Elizabeth. Almost immediately, a party opposed to him began to coalesce around Catherine. Peter III's extreme pro-Prussian policies, his great unpopularity with the military, and his refusal to embrace Orthodoxy all contributed to his overthrow on June 28, 1762. He died in captivity on July 17, presumably the victim of murder–possibly sanctioned by Catherine, who had quickly assumed leadership of the coup d'état.

Poniatowski, Stanisław August (1732–1798)

Born in what is now part of Belarus, this Polish aristocrat pursued a diplomatic career from an early age. In 1750 he encountered, in Berlin, the British diplomat Charles Hanbury Williams, who both befriended the young man and agreed to serve as his mentor in the art of diplomacy. In 1755, the powerful Czartoryski family sent Poniatowski to the court of St. Petersburg as an aide to Williams, who had been appointed as the British ambassador to Russia. Williams introduced him to the Grand Duchess Catherine–a twenty-six-year-old beauty at the time–and the two quickly became intimate. Although Poniatowski left St. Petersburg in 1758 to pursue Polish politics, he maintained a correspondence with Catherine, and he advocated a pro-Russian policy for Poland. In 1762, after Catherine's ascension to the Russian throne, he proposed marriage to her, but Catherine had other plans for him.

In 1763, Poland's King Augustus III died, whereupon the Russian empress, through a combination of diplomacy and military threat, engineered Poniatowski's elevation to the Polish throne. He was elected by the Sejm (Polish parliament) on September 7, 1764, becoming King Stanisław August.

The new king promoted cultural and political reforms in Poland, including religious tolerance, but, most importantly for

Catherine, he protested but did not actively resist the First Partition of Poland in 1772–which eventually led to the dismemberment of the country through two additional partitions (1793 and 1795). The day after the third partition was signed, November 25, 1795, Stanisław August abdicated and moved to St. Petersburg, where Catherine granted him a pension and "residence," which amounted to house arrest. He continued to advocate for Polish nationalism, but succumbed to a stroke on February 12, 1798.

Potemkin, Grigory (1739–1791)

Catherine's lover–possibly even her secret husband–and, for a time, virtually her consort, as well as commander in chief of her armies, Potemkin became the single most important *man* in the empress's Russia.

He was born in Chizevo, Belarus, of Polish extraction, the son of noble landowners. Well educated at Moscow University, he embarked on a military career, and in 1762 was in the forefront of the coup d'état that brought Catherine to the throne. She rewarded him with a small estate that year, but it was after he had distinguished himself during the Russo-Turkish War of 1768–1774 that he became not only Catherine's favorite (the fifth in that succession), a field marshal, commander in chief of the army, and governor-general of Ukraine, but also her lover. Some historians believe that the couple were even secretly married. Although the romantic aspect of their relationship ended in 1776, Potemkin remained very much within Catherine's inner political circle.

As commander in chief of the army, Potemkin revamped and modernized Russia's forces. He planned the conquest of the Crimea in 1776, and formulated many other schemes for colonization and expansion, including construction of a Black Sea fleet during 1784–1787. To support the fleet, he established an arsenal at Kherson in 1778 and a great harbor at Sevastopol in 1784.

During 1790, Potemkin successfully concluded expansionist operations against the Turks and returned to St. Petersburg, where he hoped to supplant the empress's latest (and, as it turned out, last) favorite, Platon Zubov. Catherine, however, dispatched him to Jassy to personally negotiate peace terms with the Turks. He succumbed to a fever during this mission and died.

Pugachev, Yemelyan (ca. 1742–1775)

Yemelyan Pugachev was a Don Cossack who joined the Russian army at seventeen and worked his way up the ranks to the equivalent of company commander. About 1770, he began telling fellow soldiers that he was the godson of Peter the Great, and he soon deserted the army to join dissident Cossacks who were intent on creating a community independent from Russia. Arrested for his desertion, Pugachev escaped captivity and became a fugitive.

In 1773, he began impersonating Peter III, claiming that he had escaped murder at the hands of his wife and usurper, Catherine. In this guise, he organized a band of Ural (Yaik) Cossacks in an insurgent uprising that overran a large swath of territory between the Volga River and the Urals. With great difficulty, Catherine's military forces suppressed the rebellion, which ended in a decisive battle near Tsaritsyn in August 1774. Pugachev was executed on January 21, 1775. At its height, his revolt had involved perhaps 200,000 rebels, of whom some 20,000 were killed in battle.

Saltykov, Sergei (ca. 1726–1765)

The son of a minor nobleman of an old boyar family, Sergei Saltykov was a chamberlain in the court of Elizabeth and became the first lover (and favorite) of the Grand Duchess Catherine before she ascended the throne. Catherine herself implied that her son, Paul (later Emperor Paul I), had been fathered by Saltykov, though not all historians are agreed and some have pointed out a strong family resemblance between Paul and Peter III.

Voltaire (1694–1778)
Born François-Marie Arouet in Paris, this towering figure of the French Enlightenment is universally known by his pen name, Voltaire. Remarkably prolific, Voltaire wrote some two thousand books and pamphlets in addition to conducting voluminous correspondence with major figures throughout the world, including Catherine the Great. He wrote on civil liberty, freedom of religion (and freedom *from* religion), the separation of church and state, freedom of speech, and free trade. Not surprisingly, his work had a profound influence on the American Revolution as well as the French Revolution. It was also highly influential on Catherine's understanding of the Enlightenment and inspired her own reforms of Russian government and society.

Vorontsova-Dashkova, Yekaterina (1743–1810)
Perhaps the closest female friend of Catherine the Great, Princess Dashkova was the highly educated daughter of a family prominent in the Russian imperial court and politics. She both shared and nurtured Catherine's interest in such Enlightenment authors as Montesquieu and Voltaire, among others. In 1762, the young woman became associated with those who opposed Peter III and favored the ascension of Catherine to the throne. This meant that she was also opposed to her own elder sister, Elizabeth Vorontsova, who was Peter's mistress and for whom Peter probably intended to divorce (or otherwise dispose of) Catherine.

Dashkova traveled widely and developed close relationships with numerous intellectual and cultural luminaries, including (in Paris) Benjamin Franklin, who invited her to become the first woman to join the American Philosophical Society. Catherine approved her appointment as director of the Imperial Academy of Arts and Sciences (founded by Peter the Great, and today known as the Russian Academy of Sciences), and, with Catherine, Dashkova cofounded in 1783 the Russian Academy, serving as its first president.

Williams, Charles Hanbury (1708–1759)

This Welsh-born British diplomat served as ambassador in Dresden from 1747 to 1750. While he was on a trip to Poland in 1748, he became acquainted with members of the powerful Czartoryski family and, because of this connection, came to invite young Stanisław Poniatowski to serve as his assistant when he became ambassador to Russia. It was Williams who introduced Poniatowski to Grand Duchess Catherine in 1755. This was the beginning of a romance between Poniatowski and the future empress. Williams was a frequent correspondent with Catherine.

Zubov, Platon (1767–1822)

The last of Catherine the Great's court favorites and lovers, Zubov became an enormously powerful and influential figure during the final seven years of the empress's reign. Increasingly, she consulted with him on every decision she made, and many believed that, at the height of his influence, his power exceeded even that of Grigory Potemkin in *his* heyday. The empress lavished gifts upon Zubov, including great estates and legions of serfs.

Except in his relations with Catherine, Zubov was a highly impolitic individual as well as a highly strung, even unstable, eccentric. He showed open contempt for Paul, the heir apparent, who, on his ascension to the throne after his mother's death, repaid this disrespect by relieving Zubov of his estates and all of his official posts. Paul then "advised" Zubov to leave Russia, which he did–taking up residence in Paris and Teplitz (in Bohemia) and Courland (part of present-day Latvia).

Bibliography

Alexander, John T. *Catherine the Great.* New York: Oxford University Press, 1989.

Asprey, Robert. *Frederick the Great.* New York: History Book Club, 1986.

Bain, R. Nisbet. *Peter III, Emperor of Russia.* Westminster: Constable, 1902.

Catherine II. *Memoirs of Catherine the Great.* Translated and with notes by Katharine Anthony. New York and London: Alfred A. Knopf, 1927.

Catherine II. *The Memoirs of Catherine the Great.* Edited by Dominique Maroger and translated by Moura Budberg. New York: Macmillan, 1955.

Catherine II. *The Memoirs of Catherine the Great.* Edited and translated by Mark Cruse and Hilde Hoogenboom. New York: Modern Library, 2005.

Coughlan, Robert. *Elizabeth and Catherine: Empresses of All the Russias.* New York: G. P. Putnam's Sons, 1974.

Cronin, Vincent. *Catherine, Empress of All the Russias.* New York: William Morrow, 1978.

Dashkova, Princess Catherine. *Memoirs.* London: Henry Colburn, 1840.

Dixon, Simon. *Catherine the Great.* London: Longman-Pearson, 2001.

Duffy Christopher. *Frederick the Great.* London: Routledge, 1988.

Gorbatov, Inna. *Catherine the Great and the French Philosophers of the Enlightenment.* Bethesda, Md.: Academica Press, 2006.

Haslip, Joan. *Catherine the Great.* New York: G. P. Putnam's Sons, 1977.

Madariaga, Isabel de. *Russia in the Age of Catherine the Great.* New Haven, Conn.: Yale University Press, 1981.

Massie, Robert K. *Catherine the Great: Portrait of a Woman.* New York: Random House, 2011.

Masson, Charles. *Secret Memoirs of the Court of Petersburg.* New York: Arno Press and New York Times, 1970.

Montefiore, Sebag. *Prince of Princes: The Life of Potemkin.* New York: St. Martin's Press, 2001.

Morison, Samuel Eliot. *John Paul Jones.* Boston: Little, Brown, 1959.

Oldenbourg, Zoe. *Catherine the Great.* New York: Pantheon, 1965.

Richter, Melvin. *The Political Theory of Montesquieu.* Cambridge, U.K.: Cambridge University Press, 1977.

Rounding, Virginia. *Catherine the Great.* London: Hutchinson, 2006.

Scott Thomson, Gladys. *Catherine the Great and the Expansion of Russia.* London: Hodder & Stoughton, 1947.

Smith, Douglas. *Love and Conquest: Personal Correspondence of Catherine the Great and Gregory Potemkin.* DeKalb, Ill.: Northern Illinois University Press, 2005.

Troyat, Henri. *Catherine the Great.* New York: Meridian, 1994.

Lesson Index

1 THE OUTSIDER, THE SURVIVOR, THE INSIDER

2 THE SELF-MADE MONARCH

3 THE AMBITIOUS WOMAN

4 THE STRATEGIC APPEASER

5 THE ENLIGHTENED EMPRESS

6 THE BUILDER

Index

Sterling Books by Alan Axelrod

Gandhi, CEO: 14 Principles to Guide & Inspire

Julius Caesar, CEO: 6 Principles to Guide & Inspire

Napoleon, CEO: 6 Principles to Guide & Inspire Modern Leaders

Theodore Roosevelt, CEO: 7 Principles to Guide & Inspire Modern Leaders

Winston Churchill, CEO: 25 Lessons for Bold Business Leaders

■

Profiles in Audacity: Great Decisions and How They Were Made

Profiles in Folly: History's Worst Decisions and Why They Went Wrong

■

The Real History of the American Revolution: A New Look at the Past

The Real History of the Vietnam War: A New Look at the Past

The Real History of World War II: A New Look at the Past

The Real History of the Cold War: A New Look at the Past

■

Risk: Adversaries and Allies: Mastering Strategic Relationships

Risk: The Decision Matrix: Strategies That Win